Mary,

The Lord put on my heart the desire to give you this book. It was written by my beloved mother who lost my father, almost three years ago. I have watched the Lord strengthen her as she waits on the Lord to join him in Heaven on day. I trust this will be a blessing to you.

Reneé Gandee

I NEVER KNEW HOW YOU HURT UNTIL YOUR PAIN BECAME MINE

A JOURNEY THROUGH SUFFERING AND HEALING

JOAN KNIERIM

WESTBOW
PRESS®
A DIVISION OF THOMAS NELSON
& ZONDERVAN

WestBow Press books may be ordered through booksellers or by contacting:

WestBow Press
A Division of Thomas Nelson & Zondervan
1663 Liberty Drive
Bloomington, IN 47403
www.westbowpress.com
1 (866) 928-1240

ISBN: 978-1-9736-1555-2 (sc)
ISBN: 978-1-9736-1556-9 (hc)
ISBN: 978-1-9736-1554-5 (e)

Library of Congress Control Number: 2018900910

Print information available on the last page.

WestBow Press rev. date: 02/21/2018

INTRODUCTION

Often when someone is going through troubles or a heartache, we are quick to say, "I know how you feel," but not until we have personally been touched by the same pain do we fully understand. Unless you have felt the pain of another, you really do not know how someone else is hurting. That was me. When I would speak at conferences to women and to those going through pain that I had never experienced, I often would say to them, "I know how hard this must be for you," when I had no idea what they were going through in perhaps the worst pain of their life, but *I do now!*

As a pastor's wife, I have stood with those who have had to say good-bye to a loved one for the last time, and I have expressed my love and sympathy; however, not until God suddenly called my husband home to heaven did I realize the pain, grieving, and loneliness that was ahead for me and how many widows, parents, and children are suffering with the pain of not having their loved one with them here on earth. When a loved one dies, it is not only an individual pain, but the whole family is affected. What was once a family unit has now changed. Each one will suffer differently because of what that person meant to them personally—father, mother, wife, husband, sister, brother, etc. I knew where my husband was and *Who* he was with, but the loss that was in my heart and the loneliness that came with that loss were like nothing I had ever gone through before. My husband and I had talked many times about what we would do if one of us should die before the other, but I realize now that is not something you can prepare for in advance.

Because of what I have gone through and am going through now, and because I know there are others who are walking through this same valley of pain, I asked God to show me how I could help those who are perhaps going through the worst pain of their life. Pain is no respecter of persons. We never know what the next moment or year may bring. One day we find we are in a place in life we have never been before, and we do not know what to do or how we will ever get through what has caused our pain. Our heart cries for someone to help us, and because of what I have gone through, I can say there is someone. We are not alone. There is one who is walking with us each moment and each step of the way. He has experienced every pain we may ever have.

In my pain, I began to do a complete study of what happens when someone we love dies. I wanted to know more of where my husband was. Was he alive? Was he aware of what was going on? I wanted to know for myself. I knew we had buried his body, but I also knew it was the spirit within me that was grieving. Do those who die go immediately to be with the Lord, and are they aware of all that is around them? The Bible has much to say about this, and we are not left without answers to our questions. I hope what I have found will help those who are suffering right now (whether it be through a death of a loved one or some other pain) to see that God has not left us oblivious but with complete assurance that there is help for the times when our hearts are breaking. We will get through our suffering because we have the promise of one who keeps His word—always!

I also realize that there are other pains and sufferings in the lives of many: divorce, sickness, the death of a child, having a child who is on drugs, loss of a job or a home you have worked for all your life, taking care of a loved one who no longer knows who you are, emotional and mental health issues, or pain so deep that you wonder if it will ever go away. I have seen and felt the pain others are going through when they hear the word *cancer*. Pain is all around us and is everywhere. I heard on the news recently that 13.3 suicides are committed every minute. Many people are suffering with a pain that just stays with them day and night.

All of us have times in our lives when we need to know that there is someone out there who knows what we are going through and understands and can put into words just what we need and what we are feeling. I no longer have just sympathy for others, but my pain has caused me to look into the hearts of others and feel their pain like never before.

If you are hurting ... this book is for you!

Dedicated to the glory of God and in memory of my husband, Pastor Paul R. Knierim, the most dedicated man of God I ever knew, and to my three beloved daughters, Mary Renee' Gamble, Deborah Lynn Kemp, and Rachel Joan Knierim, and to hurting hearts everywhere, whoever they may be.

CONTENTS

1

The Pain That Will Not Go Away

If you are reading this book, you may be the very one who is right now hurting with a pain that seems like it will never go away. A pastor's wife said to me just recently, "This has been the hardest year of my life." You may feel that no one understands or even cares. Perhaps it is a pain you cannot share with anyone, but you long for help. It may be a pain of having to say good-bye to one who was the dearest person on earth to you, or it may be loneliness, fear of what lies ahead, an illness, or a beloved parent or mate who lives in a world of their own, financial struggles, forgiveness to those you put your trust in and they failed you and hurt you deeply, or a pain that just stays there. People will tell you that time has a way of healing, but pain also leaves a hole in your heart and words do not take away that emptiness or fear you are feeling right now.

Often in an effort to help someone, we will say, "God knows best," which causes many to blame God and wonder why He would do this to us when it does not seem best. I am convinced God does not cause most of the things that hurt us; sin and life do! But God is with us in our pain, and He does help us through it. Perhaps a loved one was killed in an accident caused by a drunk driver. Alcohol caused the accident, not God. Or one of our loved ones was taken from us by someone who went on a shooting spree or was killed in an accident. Perhaps you have just heard the word *cancer*. Whatever has caused your pain, it hurts.

People do get sick and die from natural causes, accidents do happen, but no matter what the pain is, it seems like a part of your heart has been cut open, and it has! It is an individual and private pain, and as no two people on earth are the same, neither is suffering; but we are never alone in our worst heartache, and there is one who understands the hurt and emptiness we feel. I hope you will find what I have found; healing does come, and when it does, you realize how much God loves you and that He was caring for you in your darkest hour.

Life can be uncertain, and when sudden or lingering pain, sickness, and heartache bring us to the realization that our life or the life of someone we love will sooner or later come to an end, what then? What will we do? How will we ever get through the pain and loneliness? Some will turn to drugs, work, activity, or food or shut themselves up with their pain—anything that will help them forget for just a little while and find a peaceful place in their heart that assures them that they will be all right and will come through this. But I know for certain that those of us who turn to God will find that there was *someone* there all along who was helping us and was going through this with us and gave us a strength we did not know we had. Life happens and things can change in one moment (it did for me), but I believe (no, I know) God will take these heartaches and give us a renewed hope and peace.

I have been there, and I know there is a real God, the one and only true God who can do what we cannot do for ourselves. I am not saying that the trial will be easy, and it does not just go away overnight. The truth is that it is hard, and no matter who you are, pain hurts! But as we live moment by moment, hour by hour, day by day, and put our trust in God, call out to Him, and read and find peace in the Bible, we *will* come through! No riches can buy this, and no prescription can cure it or completely take the pain away. Pain pills may block out the pain for a time, but only Jesus can heal it completely. I hope this book will help you find the healing you so need right now.

Perhaps your pain is not one of death but of watching one you love slowly struggle with a serious illness or watching a loved one whose life has totally been destroyed by a disaster; maybe your pain is because a parent who loved and cared for you no longer knows you and has become a total stranger to you and you to them. Your pain may be because of unfulfilled dreams that you and a mate had planned to enjoy in later years of retirement together, but now their mind or body has been taken over by a disease. Maybe it is a son or daughter who has destroyed the beautiful life he or she had and is on drugs, or you may be going through a divorce and it seems there is no end to all that is going on in your life. You may see no way out, and the burden of just trying to get through one day at a time is more than you can bear. No matter what the pain is, it hurts.

I will be sharing about the death of a loved one, which is where I am right now, but no matter what is causing your pain, I believe you will find healing for your heart and soul. You may be thinking, *But you don't know my pain!* No, I do not, but I know someone who does, and He loves you and understands like no one else in all the world.

I have never been a person who struggled with loneliness or depression, but after my husband's death, there was a pain within me that had never been there before. There will come a time in all of our lives when something happens that changes our whole life. I had an emptiness within me that was like nothing I had ever experienced. As time went on, I realized that being without him was one of the hardest trials of my life. There is very little anyone can say or do to ease the pain of losing one who was a part of our life. My husband and I had been married for almost forty-nine years. Even though you may know your loved one is with the Lord, missing him or her is one of the hardest things to cope with when he or she is no longer with you. Death comes for many reasons, but when it comes, it brings with it a pain like one has never had before.

In the silence and absence of my husband's presence in an empty house, God became more real to me, and His presence began to fill each ache of my heart. As I walked through each room, sat in his chair, or read his Bible, I was without Paul, but there was an unseen presence that was comforting me. Often, we never know just how real God is until we are going through a time in our life like never before. I knew God Himself was watching over me and helping me in my time of grief. You may say, "That is because you were a pastor's wife and know what to say." No! It is because there was someone with me, comforting me, and giving me strength. God is real and is there when we need Him most. Oh, dear one, nothing in this world can compare to knowing that, even if words cannot explain it.

Death and heartache have much to teach us about life, about what really is important, about the people in our life, and about ourselves. It is perhaps one of our greatest teachers. Everyone who is part of our life leaves an impression on us, and his or her life has something to teach us. Unfortunately, we sometimes are too busy or will not take the time to learn that truth until it is too late. Death and sudden change teach us how short life is, and through our pain, we learn things we might never have learned. There comes a time in all of our lives when we need someone to lean on and to help us in what we are going through. When life takes a piece of our heart, we want to know if we are going to be all right and if life will ever be the same again. What you are feeling is normal, and others who have gone through what you may now be going through have had the same pain and thoughts. It is a part of our grieving, which in time becomes a part of our healing. There is nothing wrong with you.

Every day as you think of the one who is no longer with you, there will be new things that will bring tears. The finality of death leaves a pain like we have never had before. The grief process takes time, and we should not try to rush it. Everyone grieves and heals differently. Just remember the person who is no longer with you is still in your heart, and you are not only grieving his or her loss, but you are also grieving all of who he or she was to you and the many memories you have of him or her. You are not only saying good-bye to him or her for a time but also learning to understand what his or her absence means. So if you have to cry, then cry! It is a normal part of grieving. In time, we begin to have a deeper love for what our loved one meant to us, and these memories can never be taken away from us. We begin to cherish the little things that made our loved one who he or she was, the things he or she did and said, how he or she made us laugh, cry, and the things he or she left behind. These are the things that will stay with us forever. Our loved one will always be a part of our lives until one day when we see him or her again and then a new life will be ours together forever.

2

The Beginning of a New Life

As I am writing this, I have two friends who have recently lost a child to death. Can you imagine the pain these parents are going through? I cannot. My heart is aching for them, and even though I love and feel for them and know they have many long days and nights ahead, I do not really know what they are going through. I know what pain feels like, yes, but each of us suffers differently. Parents have told me the death of a child is one of the deepest pains a parent can have in life.

After the funeral and burial of our loved one, some of the hardest times begin. We realize our loved one is gone, and we begin to feel a loneliness like we have never known. The deep-down empty feeling is something you have never had before. You may just want to be alone and cry. Your heart longs for a peace and understanding that you will be all right. Oh, how you miss your loved one, and you now feel the emptiness of his or her being away, even though you may have known the time was coming. You feel as if your heart will break. The truth is your heart has been broken, and you wonder if the pain will ever go away. *Death and changes in our lives open our eyes like nothing else to the shortness of time here on this earth.* We begin to understand like never before that our life here is only temporary.

When our physical body dies, the Bible teaches us that our soul and spirit go to be with the Lord if we are Christians. I have found peace in knowing sickness may have taken my husband's physical body but not his soul. His soul and spirit are with God. A dear lady said to me, "When I heard about your husband, it was so sad." My reply was, "For me, yes, but not for him." The apostle Paul said in Philippians 1:23–24, "For I am in a strait betwixt two, having a desire to depart, and to be with Christ; which is far better: Nevertheless, to abide in the flesh is more needful for you." His desire was to go and be with Christ, but the people there needed him.

I can understand that. My husband was once told by doctors that six weeks to six months would be a good life for him, yet he lived fifteen years longer. Only God knows when we will take our last breath and how we will die. I believe God knew the girls and I needed him and his spiritual wisdom, and he still had a work here on earth to do for God and for others. At his funeral, many said to me, "Had Pastor Knierim given up on me, I may never have accepted Christ as my Lord and Savior, or I would not be where I am today had God not used him in my life to change me. I know he prayed for me and my family daily." Often my husband would say to me that he was not afraid to go and be with Jesus, but he knew his life here on earth was not yet finished. He spent hours praying for souls to know the Lord he knew, for pastors, missionaries, families, and their children.

No matter how others try to console us, at first, words do not seem to help. Just trying to get through each day without your loved one is one of the hardest things you will go through. Isaiah 25:8 says, "He will swallow up death in victory and the Lord God will wipe away tears from off their eyes." That is a promise we can hold on to.

Read 2 Corinthians 5:1–8 (I hope you will read all the verses, but I will quote only one). Verse 1 says, "For we know that if our earthly house of this tabernacle were dissolved, we have a building of God, an house not made with hands, eternal in the heavens." In Luke 23:39–43, two thieves were hanging on the cross alongside of Jesus. One realized that Jesus was truly the Son of God, and he saw himself for who he was and asked Jesus to remember him when He came into His kingdom. Jesus told him in verse 43, "Today shalt thou be with me in paradise."

I have every reason to believe that the day my husband died, he went immediately to be with the Lord. We may have buried his earthly body, but his spirit and soul went to be with Jesus.

Your pain may be different than mine, but God can and will heal our broken hearts when we look to Him.

3

Where Are They Now?

Since my husband's death, I have had a deeper desire to know what happens when Christians die. I would often ask him questions concerning this, and he would tell me that he believed our loved ones who had died, my mom and dad and other family members, went to be with the Lord immediately; but now I wanted to know just where my husband was. Was he aware of where he was? I know I will see him again, and heaven has become more real to me, but I wanted to know all about where he was and what God's word said about it.

We read in the Bible in Second Corinthians 5:8, "We are confident, I say, and willing to be absent from the body, and to be present with the Lord." I know that where Jesus is, that is where my husband is. I cannot imagine all that he is experiencing. He was happy here on earth, but I believe he is happier now than he ever was in his life here. Many questions began to fill my mind: Is he alive? How much does he know? Is he aware of those who have gone on before him? Can he talk with them, rejoice with them, and pray with them? With all my heart, I can say I know the answer to these questions is yes because of what I read in the Bible. In John 14:1–3 we read, "Let not your heart be troubled: ye believe in God, believe also in me. In my Father's house are many mansions: if it were not so, I would have told you. I go to prepare a place for you. And if I go and prepare a place for you, I will come again, and receive you unto myself; that where I am, there ye may be also."

I find comfort and assurance that Paul is alive, he is in the presence of the Lord, he is happier than he has ever been, and he has no pain, no suffering, and no sickness. And yes, I believe he is aware of all that is around him. My loneliness and tears are not his. I miss him so very much. I miss being able to go to him and share the things that were on my heart. He knew the word of God so much better than I did, so in my missing him and all that lies heavy on my heart, I have turned to God's word to see exactly what the Bible says about what happens when someone we love dies. Paul always said to me, "We can trust what God says in His word," and I can report today I am finding out what the Bible says about where my husband is. Sickness and death may take the body, but not the soul and spirit that lives within us. I do not doubt for one moment that his spirit went to be with the Lord to someday be reunited with his new body. What I cannot imagine is what it must have been like when he finally saw and realized that what he had preached about, looked forward to, and believed in was finally his, and there awaiting him was Jesus. There is no way I or anyone can explain the joy that is his!

One of the stories in the Bible that convinced me that my husband is in heaven and very much aware of what is going on was the story of the rich man and Lazarus. In Luke 16:19–31 both of these men had died; one went to heaven with God, and the other went to hell. The rich man could see Lazarus, and he talked to Abraham about his brothers who were still on earth. He had not forgotten his family. Now, like never before, he was concerned about them and what would happen to them when they died. He asked Abraham to send Lazarus back to them so they would not have to go through what he was now going through. He begged for Lazarus to come and just dip his fingers in cold water to ease the burning flame he felt on his tongue. Even though they both had died, the rich man knew and could see Lazarus, who was now with the Lord. I hope you will read the complete story.

Heaven is a real place, and while we are here on this earth, we need to make sure we are going to be with the Lord when we die. Hell is also real. My heart bleeds for those who do not believe this. They will believe someday, but it may be too late then.

In Luke 15:7, the Bible says, "There is rejoicing in heaven over one sinner that repenteth." Who would be rejoicing? I believe it is the saints in heaven who have gone on before us, the angels, and Jesus Himself!

Psalm 16:11 states, "Thou wilt shew me the path of life: in Thy presence is fullness of joy: at thy right hand there are pleasures for evermore." I believe my husband is healthier than he has ever been, and most of all he is in the presence of God. He can know what it is like to see Jesus. I cannot imagine what it is like for him.

Other verses that have helped me are Luke 9:27–36, Psalm 116:15, Psalm 23, Psalm 48:14, 1 Corinthians 15:54, Acts 7:55–59, Luke 24:39, Revelation 21:4, Revelation 6:9–11, Revelation 14:13, and Job 3:17. So, the Bible does not leave us without hope. It is full of assurance that our loved one is with the Lord. My sincere prayer is that you will take the time to read each of these chapters. You will be so glad you did.

On the front page of the funeral service program, our girls had a picture of their dad and written at the top were the words, "Finally Home" with the scripture verse 2 Corinthians 5:8: "We are confident, I say, and willing rather to be absent from the body, and to be present with the Lord." They truly believed their dad was finally home (John 14:1–3), and we know he is waiting for us, and he will know us, and we will know him. Because of all the promises God has left me in His word, I can face the days ahead because I know my husband is alive and with the Lord. So, to those who are suffering, there definitely is hope of seeing our loved ones again.

My husband talked about heaven, going to be with God, and all that awaited him to the point that the things of this earth became so unimportant to him. I have often wondered why pastors do not talk more of heaven and what we can expect and the joy that awaits us. People would be less fearful of death. Paul and I talked of this often, and even though he loved his life on earth, he had no fear of dying. No one could take away from him the belief that heaven was a real place, and most of all, Jesus was there.

I cannot imagine what it was like when my husband closed his eyes here on earth, and the next person he saw was the Lord. He was now in a place where there was no sin, no sickness, no shootings of little children, no bombings of planes, no taking lives of the innocent, just peace and happiness, seeing the saints of old, and praising God like never before. Sound too good to be true? Read the Bible. I have no words for all that awaits those who die and are in heaven with the Lord. Just remember that death may take the body, but it can never take the spirit and soul that lives within us. Second Corinthians 5:1 states: "For we know that if our earthly house of this tabernacle were dissolved, we have a building of God, an house not made with hands, eternal in the heaven."

Once when my husband and I were traveling, I said to him, "Honey, if you could go anywhere, where would you like to go?" Without any hesitation he replied, "Heaven!" If we all could see life that way, we would enjoy life here on earth more, and we would have more peace inside ourselves. He could enjoy life here because he had heaven to look forward to.

God cares about our pain, and He will see us through it. Yes, the pain is real, and He knows that. I believe He will use that very pain to help us in ways we could never imagine. We can look at others who have suffered and see years later how God brought them through their pain; often they are a better person than ever before. The time it takes is so hard, but it takes time to heal.

4

How Do I Get Through My Pain?

You may wonder, "Will I ever get through this pain?" The answer is yes! I am going through all of this right now, and I can say to those of you who are also going through it that it is hard—very hard. One minute you seem to be all right, but the least thing will cause you to break into tears. I can promise you the evil one will put all kinds of things in your mind: "If only I had—I wish I had taken him to another hospital, done this—said this—I should have—if only, if only." How long will it last? I do not know how long your suffering will last, but do not try to push it back. Our pain in time becomes part of our healing.

As I was writing this, it had only been a few months since my husband's death. One Sunday a man in church who sat in front of me had on a suit exactly like the one we had buried my husband in. I cried for several minutes, and all I could think of was my husband. It brought tears but also some healing and some memories. Tears can be a good thing. I saw that I could get through things that brought memories of Paul to my heart. The part of my heart that has been broken can only be healed by God; the day that my husband died, a part of me died also. Am I to be ashamed of my tears—definitely not! Pretending to be strong does not make the pain go away. Ecclesiastes 3:4 tells us there is a time to weep and mourn. There are times in our lives when it seems all we can do is cry and often that is the best medicine and cure for our heartache. So, if you need to cry—cry! You do not have to apologize for your tears. Take however long it takes for you to grieve; do not try to ignore it. Everyone is different, and there is nothing wrong with you. Your loss, whatever it is, has torn away a part of your life, and as you go about adjusting to this change and heartache, you need whatever time it takes to begin this different life you now are facing.

Another story in the Bible that has brought comfort to me is the story of Jesus crying at the grave of Lazarus. Jesus knew that He was going to raise Lazarus from the grave, yet because of His love for His friend and those suffering around Him, His heart was touched with their grief, and He cried. I know His heart is also touched with our grief, and He knows what He is going to do to help us through this very hard time of our lives, whether it be the death of a loved one or some other pain we are going through. We can trust Him! He is helping us through these dark hours far more than we can know right now. Each day we become stronger, and God gives us strength for that day.

In our sorrow, we often look back and think of all we should have said or done. Paul went so suddenly, and even though that was best for him, it was very hard for me. Had I known that morning he was going to die a few hours later, I would have been crying, sad, and telling him over and over again what a good husband and father he had been, how he was my spiritual leader, how I looked to him for so much in my life, how I needed him, and how I thanked God for the man he was to our children and grandchildren; I would have told him how I wish I could have been a better wife and how sorry I was for all the times I failed. Some know in advance that their loved one is going to die, and they can spend time sharing these things; however, some do not have that kind of time. I cannot say which way is best or easier. That is totally left in the hand of God.

My husband was not one who sought praise. In fact, he stayed away from it as much as possible. Just hours before he died, he talked to Renee' and me about his father, and he shared with us some family history that neither of us knew. The last words he uttered was to our daughter were: "I can't breathe." His next breath was with the Lord.

I would say this: Say now what you can say to a loved one and to God, even if you have said it a hundred times before. Do what you can do now and say what you can say now to bless and encourage someone. You never know what one moment or one day may bring or what it may mean to them or you later on.

When people leave us, what they leave behind becomes sacred to us: their Bible, their chair, their clothes, pictures, and who they were. Each day we become stronger, and we begin to think more about the life that lies ahead for us. *We do not always get to choose how we will die, but we can choose how we will live.* I think the thing my girls and I miss most now is the godly example and wisdom my husband had; we miss his love and our being able to go to him for advice and know he would give us godly counsel.

There is a part of my life that is empty right now without the one who was by my side for almost forty-nine years. In Hebrews 13:5, God tells us He will never leave or forsake us. I can be assured He will fill the emptiness of my life with His healing because He said He would. I may not know what my future holds, but He does, and He is guiding me to that time in my life when I will be able to find His will for me as a single.

5

Love and Pain Go Together

When I think back over the years that my husband and I had together, I have many memories of the love that our family has known. I can honestly say I know of no couple who has had the love and devotion of their children like my husband and I have had. If one of them ever heard us say that we wanted something, or if they thought of something we wanted, they would see that we got it, no matter what it cost them. Their expressions of love to us were unending. *If your parents are alive, let them know how much you love them and what they mean to you. Do for them now what you can.* In fact, do whatever you can to show them your love. Let them know what they mean to you. When they are gone, those words can never be spoken to them. Now is all we have! You may feel your parents failed you (all parents have from time to time), but if they were to die tomorrow, you will never have that time again. Do not waste the precious moments you have right now. *Parents, this is also true for your children; they need to know you love them and what they mean to you.*

My husband and I did all we could to see that our girls had what they needed (not always what they wanted), but even in all the love that surrounded our home, there was also pain. When one was ill, there was pain; there was pain when they hurt or were hurt. There was pain when they left us to go miles away to college and then when they moved miles away to begin their own family. There was pain when they had problems or heartaches, but never once did that pain cause our love to diminish. Then, the pain of seeing their dad leave this life was a pain like we had never experienced because of our love for him. There is pain in love, but I would rather have loved and had this pain than not to have had my loved ones in my life. Grieving is a sign of love. So, do not be ashamed of your grief. We do not usually grieve for those we do not love.

I think of my precious Lord and how He loved me so much that He was willing to take ridicule, beatings, mocking, and even death on the cross for me just because of His great love for me. There was pain in His life like we will never know. He came to this earth knowing He would suffer pain like no one ever had or ever will so that I might be saved. He saw that I had a need, and He was willing to die so that I might have that need met. His great love (ever so painful) made a way that my family could be together forever. John 3:16 says, "For God so loved the world that He gave His Only Begotten Son, that whosoever believeth in Him should not perish but have everlasting life." Oh, how grateful I am for that love that cost Him so much—just for a sinner like me! And dear one, you too were loved by Him just like that. I hope you will believe it and trust Him for life everlasting. First Corinthians 6:20 tells us, "We are bought with a price." The price that He paid for you and me was His life's blood. What a price to pay for us!

Because of God's love for me, He was willing to suffer pain like you and I will never know, yet He was willing to go through it because He loved me. We too will go through pain in our life, but because of the love we have for those in our family, we say, "Yes, it is worth the pain."

6

Pain Is All around Us

Of all the people in the world, each of us are individual, and no one suffers the same. Just listen to the news or read the obituaries. Many will die today or face some heartache even as I am writing this. All over the world there are hundreds of thousands of people dying every day: old people, middle-age people, young people, children, and infants. That is a lot of people crying, suffering, and grieving the loss of a loved one. Some are suffering with a pain inside them that they may not be able to share with anyone. Just think of how many people are right now getting word that someone they love has gone into eternity, has an incurable disease, was needlessly killed by someone, or is going through something that is tearing their life apart. If that is not heartbreaking, I do not know what is.

Not until we become one of those who suffer do we begin to know what others are going through; however, when we do, we become a different person, and each time we hear of a shooting, a plane crash, or a sudden death, or we attend a funeral of someone, we can honestly feel the pain that is in their heart. I may not know their particular pain, but I know what pain feels like; I have been there. Because of the pain I now have, I can watch the evening news and see the tears of someone many miles away, and I find myself crying with them. When I see a mother crying because her son has been shot needlessly, I cry for her even though we are strangers. Why? Because I know how they hurt and the pain that still lies ahead for them. My heart is connected with them because of the pain we share. Our pain teaches us more about life and living than we ever understood before.

Recently in his address to Congress, our president recognized the wife of a navy seal who was killed giving his life for our country, and as I saw the tears falling down her cheeks, her eyes looking up to heaven, I cried with her. I felt her pain, and I knew what she was trying to get through as her heart was breaking for the loss in her life. The world saw love in her pain, beauty in her tears, and because of my pain, I could cry with and for her, pray for her, and feel a kinship with her. The pain she and I have will be used to help others, and her pain certainly was used that evening, far greater than she will ever know this side of heaven! Even though we are strangers, I felt a bond with her because of our pain. She has memories none of us will ever know about her husband, such as the kind of man he was and the things that he believed in and was willing to die for; those memories will bring pain and happiness to her, sometimes all in one. *Until you have had this pain, you may feel sympathy for someone, but you do not know what they are going through.* In her pain and suffering, we saw a glimpse of the America that is still the one we know and love, one where people care for one another, feel the pain of one another, and stand for one another, some of what we may have thought was lost with so much that is going on in our world. But as people of every race, color, creed, religion, political preference, and nationality stood to their feet and applauded for the life of this young man who gave his life for our country, we saw through her pain and tears the part of America we all want to believe is still alive and great as we cried with her. All the advances in our world in technology, texting, emailing, downloading, internet, Facebook, Instagram, and the news could never do what her tears did to touch the hearts and souls of so many. We never know what our tears may do in the life of someone. I am thankful for one who, in her pain, was willing to reach out to the hearts of America like many of us will never be able to do. I hope someday I can meet her and let her know how her tears showed the world the love and pain of a wife, and in her sorrow, she reached out to those of us who are proud to be an American. A part of her husband's life and the life he left behind was still touching thousands in her display of tears and pain.

So, do not be ashamed of your tears or try to keep them back. I do not know all you may be going through, but I do know what pain feels like. All I can do is walk with you as a friend in my heart and prayers and trust our everlasting God to comfort you as only He can. We have more to look forward to than ever before. We have eternity with our loved one forever if they were a child of God!

Because of our pain, we can feel the pain and hurt others are experiencing. Even though we may not be going through the same pain, our hearts are tender toward them because of what we have or are going through. Perhaps we would never have learned this any other way. *Tears can wash away a lot of who we were, where we have failed, and open our eyes to the present and those around us; do not be ashamed of your tears. They may help us to see the hurt and pain of others and to be able to reach out to them in a way we never would have been able to before.* Good and bad comes to all of us, but God can use both the good and the bad to teach us what and who are the real values of life.

My husband would never live to see the impact his life had on so many. At the viewing and the funeral, the church halls were lined with people coming to tell me what an impact his ministry had on their life and that they were saved because he would not give up on them. There were friends, politicians, doctors' families, community and church leaders, young and old saying to me the impression his faith in God made on them. Many wrote me to say they regretted not telling him the impact he had on their life while he was alive. He never took pride in himself and always felt he could and should have done more for the Lord and others. He died in a faith he strongly trusted in, and he lived a life totally dedicated to God as much as any man could. He left me with a desire to continue the work he gave his life to: prayer, staying in the word, and service to God.

Perhaps this is the way God plans it. Many of the great servants of God were not known until after their death, and then we read and hear about who they were and the life they gave for the cause of Christ. My husband would be the first to say if his life brought praise to God, that is how it should be, not to himself. I have asked myself since his death, "Just how much of my life is giving glory and praise to God?"

God is working in our lives constantly to bring us into a deeper understanding of who He is and to show us how much He loves us and wants to use us in all of our life here on earth. The pain we may be going through today is multiplied by many all over the world, and many will suffer pain far worse than we will ever know or experience. We can trust Him to see us through because He makes this promise all through the Bible. He cannot and will not lie—*ever*!

7

Will My Pain Ever End?

Your loved one will always be with you in your heart. Your life has changed, and change is not always easy to deal with. You will learn to live with their absence, but they will always be within you. No two people will grieve the same way, so do not think of others who have gone through what you are now going through and think you should be like them. Others may say, "You'll get through this," but at the time, these words do not comfort because you are hurting now. Perhaps some of the things that have helped me most will also help you.

As time goes on, you begin to remember and cherish all the memories of your loved one. These very memories can bring healing to you, so do not push them away, even if it hurts as you think on them. I realize many do not have special memories, and I am so sorry for that. But remember—no one is perfect, and we all have things in our life we wish we had done differently. Do not dwell on those times; think of the good times. The evil one will do everything he can to make you think of memories that are not so special, but neither God nor your loved one would want you to think that way.

My husband took care of me. Although his body was weakened and he could not do a lot of things around the house, he still took care of me. If every husband could leave this legacy to a wife, what a jewel is hers! He taught me by his life and example that we could always trust

God. Every day we would pray together, and I would hear him first of all praise and thank God for the great salvation we had in Jesus. Then, he would begin to pray for others, such as family members, church members, pastors, missionaries, and people near and far away. Oh, could he pray! I must admit there were times I would think, *How could he have so much to pray for when he had already been up early praying?* Now, if I could only hear him pray again, how my heart would rejoice. One of the very best things we can do for someone is to pray for them. He prayed for our president, our country, and so many others who were on his heart.

He always wanted me to have the best, and yet his desires were very few. He made sure I would be cared for in case something happened to him, and his desire was for our girls to "watch out for your mother." After his death, I found out plans he had made years in advance to make sure I was cared for in case he went to heaven before I did. That was him, never wanting praise, just going about doing good. If you have and were blessed with someone like that in your life, make sure you thank God daily for that gift. So often we take those around us for granted until they are no longer with us. John 15:13 says, "Greater love hath no man than this, that a man lay down his life for his friends." Jesus did that for us, and I know my husband would have given his life for me and our daughters.

There were so many things I still had to tell him, to talk to him about; but no matter how much time we have, when our loved ones are gone, we wish we had more. We are never really ready for them to leave. That is why we need to do what we can now and cherish the moments we have now, especially with our loved ones. Whether it be a child, parent, husband, or anyone close, when they are gone, their presence will always be with you in what they did for you, meant to you, said to you, and what they left behind. Do not push these memories aside; cherish them.

I am thankful there is one who is going through this with me and knows my pain like no other. Grieving does not show a lack of faith. If you are a Christian, you grieve but not without hope because you know someday you will see your loved one again (First Thessalonians 4:13).

Even in our hope, the pain is still real. Death makes us see more than ever that this world we are living in is not the end and that it will not last forever, but we have a future hope in a life to come that will never end. We have God's promise that He will not leave us comfortless and that He will come to us (John 14:18).

I am afraid many live as if this is the only life they will have, when in reality this life is just a stop-over to life everlasting. Many fail to believe this, but that is why Jesus came and died. If ever I wished I had words to tell everyone who is reading these words to make sure they know where they will spend eternity, it would be now. Everyone is going to die, sooner or later, and we will either spend life everlasting with God in the new heaven and new earth or in hell forever. This is a truth the devil does not want us to know. Who are we going to believe, God or the devil? John 5:28–29 says, "Marvel not at this: for the hour is coming, in the which all that are in the graves shall hear His voice, And shall come forth; they that have done good, unto the resurrection of life; and they that have done evil, unto the resurrection of damnation."

Because of our pain, we can now feel the pain and hurt others are feeling. Even though we may not have gone through the same thing they are going through, we know what it feels like when they are facing something that has come into their life and is breaking their heart like nothing ever has. God is the only one who can best comfort us in our time of sorrow; whether we believe it or feel His presence, He is with us in every pain. He knows, and He can and will restore that aching heart. Others may be there to comfort and help us, but only God can see the inside of us. You and I have never been where we now are in our life, but Jesus has, and He has walked ahead of us. He knows how to help us get through this pain and bring peace to our heart and soul. Yes, you are grieving and the pain you now have will end, but you will always have the memory of your loved one in your heart, and it is a memory you never want to lose.

8

A Beautiful Picture of Death

My grandson Michael made a statement about his great-grandma Gamble, who is in her nineties and is critically ill. When I asked him how his grandma was, he said, "She is going to heaven, but we just don't know when she will be leaving." She was ready to go, and he understood that. He just did not know when she was leaving. What a beautiful picture he painted of death and leaving this world. That is our life; we all are going to take a journey and die, but we just do not when we are going to leave.

My husband studied the Bible so intensely, and he believed every word he read. He was confident that death to a Christian could never take the spirit, the heart, and the soul, and even though the body may lay in a grave, the soul lives on forever and greater and more joyful than ever before. We may write about heaven and talk about heaven, but there are no words that would even come close to what awaits us.

Second Corinthians 5:1–8 tells us that while we are here on earth in our earthly bodies, we are absent from the Lord, but when we leave this body, we go to be with Him. I believe the moment my husband took his last breath here on earth, he was in the presence of Jesus. It is so important that we tell everyone we can about how they too can go to heaven. If not heaven, the Bible teaches that hell awaits those who reject Jesus as their Savior. There are many today who do not want to hear this and may even make light of it, but someday they will wish they had believed it.

Many a time right before someone dies they may say they see the Lord or angels coming for them. In the Acts 7:59, Stephen called out, "Lord Jesus, receive my spirit." Even though they killed his body, they could not kill his soul. He did not ask Jesus to receive his body but his spirit, the heart and soul of who he really was.

When I think of where my husband is, I no longer think of him lying in a cold grave. I think of him being in heaven and talking with the saints of old, with family and friends and happier than he had ever been here on earth. Will we know one another? Yes! After the death and resurrection of Jesus, many of His disciples and friends saw and knew Him. The Bible tells us we will be known as we are known. In Luke 24:39, Jesus said to them, "Behold My hands and my feet, that it is Myself." They were told to touch Him and see that He was real flesh and blood. I truly believe my husband will know me and our daughters when we are joined with him forever in heaven. The life there will be so glorious and so perfect and the love so great that we cannot imagine what it will be like. We will have God's love, and that love will transcend to everyone in heaven like nothing we ever experienced here on this earth.

If you will look up all the scriptures listed, I believe you too will see that there is a new life waiting for us. This life here on earth is just one we are traveling through on our way to life everlasting. Read the book of Revelation, especially the twenty-first chapter, and see what awaits those who know Jesus Christ as their Lord and Savior. There is a wonderful life ahead for those who have put their faith and trust in the Lord Jesus for the forgiveness of sin. My husband was not afraid to leave this life for the one he now enjoys. Death ends this earthly life, but it is the beginning of a new life forever for the Christian who has accepted Jesus as their Lord and Savior. What a comfort this is to our grieving heart.

So often we worry about what will happen to us here, and we fail to realize (and many do not believe) this world is only for a short time. The Lord *is* going to return, and it could happen when we least expect it—the Bible tells us in a "twinkling of an eye." Just think how quick a blink of an eye is. We will not have time then to decide to follow Jesus.

We need to make preparation now! It is sad when so many today live as if this is the only life they will have. They will find out one day that Satan fooled them, and it will be too late then.

First Corinthians 2:9 says, "But as it is written, eye hath not seen, nor ear heard neither hath entered into the heart of man the things which God hath prepared for them that love Him." One of my favorite songs is "In the Sweet By and By."

> There's a land that is fairer than day
> And by faith we can see it afar,
> For the Father waits over the way
> To prepare us a dwelling place there.

Knowing our loved ones are present with the Lord is a comfort to those of us who remain on earth. Our life here is just preparation for the life to come. *We get so busy living life here, we sometimes forget this life will not last forever.* There is a new world that will last forever, and that is the life we need to be most concerned about and making sure we will live there.

When my husband and I would travel to see our girls and we would get back home, he would say many times, "It's good to be home." And, sometimes when we were away he would say, "I'm ready to go home." Well, he definitely was ready for his heavenly home, and I believe that is where he is—finally home! My heart has found a resting place in knowing this.

I cannot imagine when my husband arrived *home* how happy he was. I believe there was a crowd to meet him and welcome him home, and to see the face of the one he loved and served here on earth must have been joy unspeakable. And he was able, for the first time in many years, to get down on his knees and worship the Lord. What makes me believe this? God's word. Matthew 24:35 tells us that this old world will pass away, but God's word will never pass away.

Someday the trumpet will sound, our Lord will return, and the body of our loved one who has been asleep will come out of the grave to join the Lord. Read 1 Thessalonians 4:13–18. These verses tell us what we can expect when the Lord Himself comes again for us. I am not able to explain all that will happen, but I do believe God's word, and I know what God says He will do. Revelation 21:4 says, "And God shall wipe away all tears from their eyes, and there shall be no more death, neither sorrow, nor crying, neither shall there be anymore pain: for the former things are passed away." For those who have put their faith in Jesus, we have a new life ahead forever and forever. Just think of that—no more pain, no suffering, no sickness, no troubles or heartaches, forever with the Lord Jesus and our loved ones. Doesn't make death so fearful, does it?

Finally Home

Rev. Paul R. Knierim
November 27, 1942—November 28, 2015

We are confident, I say, and willing rather to be absent from the body and to be present with the Lord.—2 Cor. 5:8

9

In Your Pain Reach Out to Others

You may not feel you are ready to reach out to others, but this too will help you in your grieving. They are all around us; in the grocery stores, at church, everywhere we go there are people who are hurting. They may be right in our home. I purposely began to look for others who seemed sad and people who needed to know someone noticed them. It may be someone we could send a note to or do something for. When things hung heaviest on my heart, I would get in the car and ask God to lead me to someone I could encourage or help. I would just go out and look for others who might need a word to lighten their heart that day—a clerk, a stranger, someone at church, in the market—they are all over. People are hurting, and a good word from you can make their day. It can also help you.

We cannot see or know the grief others are carrying. We cannot look into their souls, hearts, and minds and see what they are going through like God can, but we can show kindness and love to them and tell them of God's love. Many who are in our very midst are carrying heavy burdens that they can tell to no one. I ask God every day to put in my heart and my life those I can help. He always does!

Realizing how quickly our life can (and often does) change in a moment's time made me realize all I have is right now. My husband's life here on earth and his life in going to heaven made me want to know and do the will of God like never before, because now is all I have. When he was alive, I would go to him with my concerns, and he always gave me godly advice. We would pray together and seek God's will for whatever burdens we had. Now, as a single person, I still can look to the one who will meet the needs of my life and loneliness like never before. So each time I can be an encouragement and point others to Jesus, I think, *The witness and work of my husband still lives on in the lives of those I am able to touch because of his influence in my life.* My life should show the influence of God in me.

When we come to the end of life, what is it that really matters? God and people. Life changes moment by moment and day by day. Life is for now, and the people God gives us as family and friends are the true treasures of life—the only treasures here on earth we can take to heaven with us. We do not know if we will have tomorrow, but how we live life today can brighten the present and the future. John 10:10 tells us the devil comes to steal, kill, and destroy. Jesus comes that we might have more of life. He wants us to be happy and at peace. The devil wants to steal our happiness and joy. He will do all he can to place fear and doubt in our hearts. Jesus wants us to enjoy life here and prepare for life forever with Him.

My husband had a peace with God like no one I ever knew, and he had peace here on earth no matter where we were or what we were doing. I am convinced that is one reason he lived longer than doctors said he would. He always told me he was convinced our health was hurt more by what we let *eat at us* than *what we ate*! Paul had learned how to leave all to God's care, whether it was his health, his life, his peace, or his faith. His whole life, moment by moment, was in the Lord's hand. I must admit I do not always have a peace like that. When we would pray about something that concerned our family, he would say, "Joan, God will take care of it; let's just wait and see what He is going to do." He not only trusted God for the present but for the future also. He had the faith of a little child (Matthew 18:1–4). He learned to leave the past, the present, and the future in the hand of his God. One day, years ago, the doctor came into his hospital room and told him he may not have many days ahead because his health was so bad. He sat up in bed and quoted Psalm 118:24: "This is the day which the LORD hath made; we will rejoice and be glad in it." And, he did exactly that!

When Jesus taught his disciples to pray "give us this day our daily bread," it was not bread for tomorrow or next week, but for today. We need to pray for God to give us the strength for today, and He will. My husband lived like that, and we can too when we trust God to take care of our needs.

10

Helps to Healing

1. *Cry.* Do not try to hold back the tears and try to be strong. Whether it be because of sickness, death, divorce, family problems, or whatever is bringing pain to you, cry if you have to. Jesus cried when He went to the grave of his dear friend Lazarus. Even though He knew He was going to raise Lazarus from the grave, He hurt in His heart with sadness and love for His friend and for those around Him. I am a crier. Tears have a way of cleansing our hearts and souls. Perhaps God gives us tears to help relieve the pain of our hearts and to open our eyes to what really is important in life.

2. *Let others take over where they can.* My three girls stepped in for me (even though their hearts were breaking), and I went to the viewing, to the funeral, and through the days ahead with their help. They helped me select the clothes for their dad (and me), the display pictures, and funeral video. Letting your children be part of this can be good for them and you. This can be true of other pains. So often, we hide our deepest pain from our children, trying not to cause them worry or stress. They can be stronger than we might realize, so let them help.

3. *Be with others after the funeral for as long as you need to.* If you have family and children who invite you to go be with them for

a few days, do it! I went to be with each of my girls, and even though we cried much, we were together for weeks. I knew I had a lot of decisions to make, but I did not need to do it right away.

4. *Talk about your loved one.* Express how you miss them and how you feel. Do not be ashamed of your grief; you do not need to try to be tough and strong. Grief is not a sign of weakness; it is called *love*! Others may shy away from talking about your loved one, fearing it might cause you more pain. Talking about your loved one will not only help you but help others also. Do not be afraid to laugh; you are not being disrespectful. There were many things in your life that brought laughter, so do not push these out of your mind. Laughter as well as tears is a part of healing.

5. *Draw close to God.* At first my prayer was, "Lord, I need Your help." There was so much going on in my heart and mind with people coming and going that I was unable to read my Bible or pray like I did before. There were days I felt like a zombie, but I found out that God gave me strength I did not know I had. He understood all I was going through. Later on, my Bible reading became even more precious than ever. In my weakness, my loneliness, and the absence of my husband, I spent hours in the Bible. God spoke to my heart about where my husband was and who he was with. This brought great comfort to my aching heart. Do not stay away from church. If you are not a churchgoer, now is a good time to begin. Other Christians will be a strength and encouragement to you.

6. *Do not rush any decisions.* It is hard to get used to your new role in life as a single person. Do not rush it. For almost forty-nine years, it had been the two of us. You do not have to be on a time schedule in your grief. It is a difficult time really, or it was for me, and each day it became harder as I would go through the house and see how much his absence left behind. My husband had so much wisdom, and I depended on him for that. A good example of this is that even though we had a GPS for directions in our car, we never used it. He always directed me better than

any GPS. I very seldom traveled without him, but when I did, he wrote everything out for me. Now I had to learn to either travel by myself or stay put until one of the girls came for me. I kept hearing him say to me, "Joan, God will lead you and help you in anything you need; just ask." I have asked, and He has helped me! I have traveled to visit our girls, and I now use the GPS. This may seem like a simple thing to some, but God is concerned about the small things as well as the big things in our life.

7. *Take as long as you need to adjust to your life now, and do not feel guilty.* Many who have had loved ones die, or have gone through a heart-wrenching change, have advised me not to make any serious decisions that I do not have to make for at least a year or longer. If you do it too soon, you may make decisions you will be sorry for later.

8. *Pray.* If you are not a Christian, now is the time to put your trust in God. Someday when all the pieces come together and we see the big picture of our life, we will understand why, and we will know God was with us in all we went through on earth to bring us into our new eternal life with Him. *In time, we may learn that our tears taught us more how to live than all the happy times we were privileged to have.*

   Deuteronomy 29:29 says, "The secret things belong unto the Lord our God: but those things which are revealed belong unto us and to our children for ever, that we may do all the words of this law." There are some things that we may never understand here on this earth, but there are so many precious truths and promises in the Bible we can know and understand for sure.

9. Talk to someone who has gone through your pain. Not only will you get help, but you just may find a new friend to walk with you in your pain.

10. *Take one day, one week, one month* at a time; peace and help come slowly, but they do come!

11. *Make sure you know how to handle personal business.* I hope your husband leaves you with instructions on what to do. (Women

need to do this for their husband and children, telling them where to find things, etc.) I had to check our will, have the titles to our cars changed, change over our bank account, insurance, etc. He had told me many times what to do and I listened, but I never really soaked it in because I knew he was there. Here again, do not rush anything or try to do it all at once; just take one step at a time. If you do not understand everything, let your children help you or get a professional person to help with the taxes, personal finances, etc. I had a dear friend and a niece who were financial advisors, and they were able to help me in so many decisions.

12. *Learn now* about electric, plumbing, water, gas, changing the filter on the furnace. It was all new to me on what to do and who to call. Learn to do it now if you can.

13. *Make sure you have copies of death certificates.* You will need several copies of the death certificate. Make sure you have the funeral director order these for you. There will be a charge, but it is something you will need.

14. *Decide now about organ donation.* If your loved one wants any of their organs donated to help someone, make sure you are aware of this. Hopefully, the hospital will ask you right away; ours did not. In the shock of my husband's sudden death, I forgot he wanted to donate any part of his body that someone else could use. They never asked me. What a shame because his eyes, liver, or perhaps something else could have helped someone, and Paul would have wanted that.

15. *Make funeral arrangements in advance.* My husband had made arrangements and paid for our funeral in advance, so all we had to do was meet with the funeral director and set a time for the viewing, the funeral, pick out his clothes, etc. You will need to know what you want in the obituary. Our funeral director took care of this for me such as submitting it to the local newspapers, and printing the program for the funeral. Just remember that there will be some extra expenses even though you may have paid for the funeral arrangements years in advance. The funeral

director was a personal friend of ours, and he went out of his way to make things easier for us. My husband had already chosen the casket he was to be buried in. He had designed the inside lining, which represented his life verses and his faith in God. *Some other things that were a help in my healing:*

16. *Cherish acts of kindness.* So many people sent me cards and notes telling me how my husband had influenced their life. This was a blessing to me. One young man, Daniel Armacost, who grew up in our church and the Christian school sent me a three-page typed single-spaced letter listing many things he remembered about my husband and the impression he made on his life as a young man growing up. I have read this over and over. Another young man, Darien Templeton, who also grew up in the church and school and is now a captain in the military, sent me some pictures of my husband with some of the kids from the church and school. He also sent me a military medallion expressing to me how my husband had made a difference in his life.

   A dear friend Tami Beverly sent me a note telling me that each time she and her husband went to visit my husband when he was in the hospital to encourage him, they came away encouraged because of how he talked about me and his love for me. Can you imagine how this helped me? Believe me—I was far from perfect and failed in so many ways, which he and I both knew, yet his love for me never diminished. True love never ends no matter how we may fail, and I sure did that enough! Wayne Beverly, a deacon in our church, wrote a tribute poem about my husband and had it framed for me. These and many other acts of kindness helped with my grieving and are things I look at and read often. It has caused me to be more aware of others who are suffering and to say and do what I can to be a blessing to them. We can learn how to help others by the things that helped us.

17. *Friends.* We had several family and friends who drove hundreds of miles to be at my husband's viewing and funeral to encourage us. This was at the Christmas season, which is one of the busiest

times of the year, yet they came. Just their presence and sacrifice meant more to us than any words could ever say. If you are reading this and want to know how you can help others who are going through a heartache, a death, or something else, just be there for them. That is one of the best things you can do. Do not worry about saying the right thing; you do not have to say anything. Later, you may want to send them a note telling them you are there and how they or their loved one touched your life and that you are praying for them and care about them.

18. *Record your thoughts and prayers.* My daughter Lynn gave me a prayer journal, and I would write out my prayers to God and many times my thoughts to my husband as if he were there right beside me. This may seem silly to some, but it helped me.

19. *Allow time to say good-bye.* The hardest of all at this time is saying good-bye. Later as you miss your loved one and begin to go on with your life, you will take another step in healing, but let sorrow do its work and let God give you the strength you need. The journey of grief is different for everyone, so do not feel you are weak or try to be extra strong.

20. *Watch out for the guilty feelings.* I can promise you they will come. The devil will do all he can to make you feel guilty and make you think, *If only I had done more.* We need to let these feelings go, move forward, and not look back as we all are tempted to do. As I have said before, the past is gone forever and the present will end sooner than we think it will. Cherish the good times and special moments. Do not let the evil one fill your mind with the "what ifs." The one who is gone would not want you to do this. Perhaps God allows us to see where we think we failed to cherish every moment with our loved ones and say what we need to say now! Revelation 20:10 tells us that the devil knows what awaits him, and he will do all he can to deceive us and take away our peace. John 10:10 says, "The thief cometh not, but to steal, and to kill, and destroy: I am came that they might have life, and that they might have it more abundantly."

21. *Understand friends are trying to help.* Others mean well when they say, "If I were you," so do not be offended by their remarks. They are trying to find words that will help you. They are not you, and you need to do what is best for you and grieve in your own way and do what you think you should do.

22. *Continue family celebrations,* holidays, anniversaries, and special times with your children and grandchildren. Celebrations can all be very hard because you know how much this would have meant to your loved one who is no longer with you. I choose to think of where my husband is and that he is so much happier than me. He would have wanted me to be part of all these celebrations even if he were here and could not make it because of his health.

One day I had purchased something for myself, and I thought, *I wish I had done this for Paul.* It was almost as if the Lord spoke to me and said, "You think for one minute anything you have here on earth is better than what he has now?" That thought has carried me through a lot of "I wish I had done this for him" and realizing he would not have wanted me to anyway because things meant very little to him.

These are things that not only will help us in our healing but are things we can do to be a help to others who are suffering. You may think of other ways that helped you. Write them down. You never know when those very things may be what will be used to help someone else when they are going through the pain you are now going through. Don't be concerned if you should or should not do something. No matter how small it may seem to you, just do it.

11

You Will Come Through

The hardest on me was when my girls would cry. They loved their dad so much, and he sure did love them! I tried to help them, but I could not. We just need to let our children grieve their own way and be there for them when they need to talk or cry. Our hearts were grieving for his absence, but we were rejoicing that he was with the Lord, to never know sickness or death again.

Many say getting through the first year is the hardest. You may have just come through the year without your loved one, yet you still cry at times. Do not think something is wrong with you if you still have days of loneliness and tears. You do not wake up on the 366th day and think, *It's been a year, and I should be over this.* I never want to get over my husband and forget all that he meant to me and the difference his presence made in my life. Sometimes just the thought of him will bring tears to my eyes. Again, I emphasize it is not a sign of weakness, so do not feel you are weak or have a lack of faith.

My greatest strength came from God and a verse in Isaiah 41:10. Also, my eight-year-old granddaughter, Morgan, stayed right by me, and whenever she saw me cry, she would come and just stand near me and hold my hand. Her papa would have been so pleased with that. Actually, it was the little things that gave me a lot of comfort and still does. My nineteen-year-old grandson, Michael, sat with me and kept looking out for me, watching over me, and helping me. Our other grandson, Mitchell, shared at the funeral what his papa's life had taught him. You may be surprised how a child can be a wonderful strength at this time. Lauren and Bethany and all our grandchildren had Mitchell read their thoughts of their papa at the funeral. This was their way of saying good-bye to their papa.

Accept your weakness. I wanted to be strong and take care of my girls when actually I needed them to take care of me. When our girls said, "Mom, we know Dad would want us to take care of you and help you right now," I felt a sense of relief in just letting go and forgetting to be a mother for a while and just letting them help me. By doing so, we were helping one another. Each of them did all kinds of things for me by having me in their home for weeks at a time, waiting on me, even though they were suffering also.

Do not get upset if you forget a lot of things. Realize you are not thinking like you did before the death of your loved one (or any drastic change in your life). I had to make lists because I forgot things I never forgot before. In making a list, I had in front of me what I had to do. Also, when you forget things, do not begin to think you are losing it.

Your mind as well as your whole body is going through a change. Do not feel you have to decide right now on the things you are not sure about; just take one day at a time. Ask God what you are to do next. No one knows my future but God. We can trust Him to lead us into the unknown. As I trust Him today, He will give me the wisdom and strength for that day. Proverbs 3:5–6 says, "Trust in the LORD with all thine heart and lean not unto thine own understanding. In all thy ways acknowledge Him, and He shall direct thy paths." God can and will speak to us on critical decisions we have to make.

At nights, I wore my husband's pajamas when I was alone at home. This may sound silly to some, but I felt closer to him. Sometimes it helped me to write out my thoughts as if Paul were there. I would often write out my prayers to God. Whatever helps you, that is what you should do; do not worry about what someone may think or whether you should or should not be doing this. If you cannot cry, do not feel something is wrong with you. We all grieve differently.

Going back to what you did together, it was hard the first time I went back to church and sat in the pew he and I always sat in. I cried during most of the service, but everyone was kind and understanding. People really are caring.

Be aware of the evil one, who will put all kinds of thoughts in your head. If we allow sadness and regrets to remain in our lives for a long period of time and listen to Satan's poisonous thoughts, life and sorrow becomes even harder to deal with. Everyone has regrets. We must trust God with our failures. The Bible tells us God will keep us in His peace when our mind is stayed on Jesus. That does not mean I walk around 24–7 telling myself to think about Jesus. What it does mean to me is that deep in my heart, I know God is always with me, and I have a settled peace knowing I can trust Him for the strength I need each day. I have found this to be true, and I try to think good thoughts instead of sad thoughts. Philippians 4:8 says, "Finally, brethren, whatsoever things are true, whatsoever things are honest, whatsoever things are just, whatsoever things are pure, whatsoever things are lovely, whatsoever things are of good report; if there be any virtue, and if there be any praise, think on these things."

In my indecisions of not knowing what to do, verses like Isaiah 43:18–19 helped me: "Remember ye not former things, neither consider the things of old. Behold I will do a new thing now, it shall spring forth; shall ye not know it? I will even make a way in the wilderness, and rivers in the desert." I found peace in knowing God knows the way through this wilderness I am going through, and He will lead me through it. My prayer was, "God, I need your peace in what I am to do (Psalm 29:11). Am I to stay in Ohio or move down South and be near our girls? What is Your will, and where am I to go from here? How am I to honor You and my husband's life?" You pray your own prayer; this is just how I prayed. God gave me Psalm 34:18–19: "The Lord is nigh unto them that are of a broken heart and saveth such as be of a contrite spirit. Many are the afflictions of the righteous; but the LORD delivereth him out of them all." God has done this for me.

Do not stay away from others or close yourself up alone in a dark room or house. Get up and get out—life goes on. Go for a walk, exercise, go shopping. At the time of my husband's death, I had just undergone complete spine surgery and two hip replacements and was using a walker. Long walks and exercise were not an option for me, but I could talk on the phone and encourage others, write notes, etc. The main thing is not to stay shut off by yourself. It was at this time I began to write this book, sharing with others what helped me and how they can help others who are going through a painful time in their life. When family and friends invite you out, do it!

When you do not know what to do, just wait! That is such a little word, but when we do come through the dark times, we will know that God was there all along, guiding us and giving us wisdom we did not know we had. Often we want to talk to someone, but the One we need to get alone with and listen to is that still, small voice from God. He speaks to us through His Holy Spirit within us. If there is a friend, family member, or someone you want to talk to, do it, this is also helps in our healing.

When we come through the darkness of life, no matter what it is, we learn in a greater way what trusting God can do, what He will do, and what He has done for us. God promises never to leave or forsake us when we go through the valleys, and we can trust in His promise. If we come through these painful times *bitter* instead of *better*, I doubt we have allowed God to speak to us at all. Our God does not leave us. When you put your trust in God, you will come through it and you will find, as I have, the sun will shine again and your tears will find laughter again and that He was there with you all along.

In Second Corinthians 1:3–4 we read, *"Blessed be God, even the Father of our Lord Jesus Christ, the Father of mercies, and the God of all comfort: Who comforteth us in all our tribulation, that we may be able to comfort them which are in any trouble, by the comfort wherewith we ourselves are comforted of God."* Paul the apostle could talk like this because of all he had been through and seen. When you and I have experienced what others are going through, we have a deeper understanding, and we can tell them what we know God will and can do in our deepest need no matter what it is. Believe me, the evil one is real, and he will do all he can to cause us to doubt, fear, and lose hope that we will come through the deepest pain of our heart. We have God's promise He is with us. *There is a brighter day ahead.*

Death leaves a place in our heart that in time will heal, but death can never take away from us the love we have in our hearts because love is forever. Our suffering, whatever the reason, is always an unwelcome part of life which no one likes. All through history we read of the pain and suffering many have gone through and some may say, "Why?" Why does God allow some of the worst things to happen to good people when He could have prevented it from happening. We must remember suffering is a part of our life here on earth, and those who blame God instead of looking to God destroy themselves along with their pain. Our pain does not have the last say in our life; the empty tomb and cross is our victory. God was there when His Son was nailed to the cross. He was there when Jesus was spat upon, laughed at, and mocked; He was there when Jesus cried out, "My God, why have you forsaken me?" and He is with us now.

The words to the song "Even in the Valley God is Good" was a comfort to me.

High upon the mountain
The sun is shining bright
My heart is filled with gladness
Here among the cares of life

But I've just come through the valley
Of trouble fear and pain
It was there I came to Know my God
Enough to stand and say

Even in the valley God is good
Even in the valley He's faithful and true
He carries His children through
Like He said He would
Even in the valley God is good

This road of life has lead you
To a valley of defeat
You wonder if the Father
Has heard your desperate plea

But there's hope in that rugged place
Where tears of sorrow dwell
Can't you hear Him gently whispering
I'm here and all is well

Even in the valley God is good
Even in the valley He's faithful and true
He carries His children through
Like He said He would
Even in the valley God is good.
Author: Rebecca J. Peck & Amy Marie Zika
Used by permission

12

How to Help Those Who Are Hurting

You may not be the one suffering right now but wondering what you can do to be of help to those who are suffering. I will list a few things that were a help to me and how we can be of help to others in their pain.

* Tell them you are praying for them, and do it! Ask God to give them the strength that only He can give. When my sisters, Mary Lou, Geri, and Tennie, and my brothers, DJ, Harry, and others, told me they were praying for me, I knew they were doing just that.

* Be there for them. If there is a viewing and funeral, be there! Just seeing the many who came showed me more than any words could say that they cared and were there to encourage and support our family. No matter what the pain someone is going through, be there for them. People may not remember what you said, but they will remember how you made them feel just by your presence.

* You do not need to offer advice of what they should or should not do. All they need is just to know you care.

* Do not be concerned about what to say. Just your being there will be something they will get strength from now and later. We do not need to have the right words. Just your presence speaks louder than any words. All you simply have to say is something

like: "I know you're hurting right now, and I hurt with you. I'm going to be here for you." If you have gone through what they are now going through, it is only natural that you want to help them, but there will come a time in days ahead when they may need to talk with you more, and your words will have more meaning to them then; or, they may need you just to listen.

* Show compassion to those who are grieving. Our girls told me that at the casket, as we were saying our last good-byes to their dad, our pastor had tears in his eyes. They will never forget this and even though I was not aware of it, we will always remember his love for their dad and his grieving with us. No sermon could have said more! His tears meant more than words to our girls at that time.

* If you know someone can use food, make him or her a meal; help with cleaning, or picking up family from the airport. You can stop by their home and do what you can, but if the family is there with them, do not feel you have to stay. They may need this time alone just to talk and to be together.

* If the person is alone and has no family, this may be the time to ask if he or she would like for you to stay with them, take him or her to the funeral home, etc. You will know what to do if he or she needs you to do something for them.

* Continue to check on your friends who are suffering. Often, weeks after the funeral, cards, flowers, and phone calls begin to let up, but their pain is still very deep—even a year or more afterward. Do not hesitate to send a card or note just saying, "I'm thinking of you, and if there is something at all I can do, I want to do it."

* If they are alone, stop by their home or call and offer to take them to lunch or shopping; just listen to them, or even cry with them.

* Do not be afraid to talk about their loved one, especially if they have been a blessing to you. If you have some fond or funny memory of their loved one, say it! It may be just what they need to hear. You will know what to say, and they will too. Even

46

though I cried every time I talked about my husband, it was healing for me. It did not mean I was depressed, nervous, or even lonely; most of the time it was just because my heart was still so tender missing him and trying to get through the day without him.

* Send cards, texts, or emails of encouragement. The same young man who sent me a three-page letter after my husband died, telling me things he remembered about him when he attended the Christian school and church my husband pastored, sent me another letter a year later. This was a busy young man in the ministry and he had a family, yet I knew he was thinking of my husband and me.

* Your presence at the beginning means so much, but the fact that you still care months and years later mean even more.

* Offer to help where you can, cut grass, and help with household things they may not be able to do themselves. A couple, Bill and Faydean Bell, did many things for me around the house I was unable to do. What a blessing this was to me.

* If you are a medical professional, take time with your patients who are hurting. My doctor, Dr. Gabriel Maijub, and his nurse practitioner, Alisha Mills, both were a great help. Most do not have a doctor who is their friend like Paul and I had. The first time I went for my regular checkup after Paul's death, they took extra time with me, hugging me, and letting me cry. They did not make me feel like I was depressed or having a nervous breakdown, but they expressed what a good husband I had and how he took care of me. If more doctors would show this type of compassion, it would make all the difference in their patients healing physically, emotionally, and spiritually. Some may feel they do not have the time, but the truth is, they would be the talk of the town and would have to keep adding more staff to their practice because of patients telling others.

* People may not remember what you said, but they will remember how you made them feel just by your presence. One night in church, a soloist sang "Look for Me at Jesus's Feet" and I began

to cry. My dear friend, Floris Dunaway just put her arm around me during the song. She never said a word, but her love and compassion said more than any words could say. Just do what your heart tells you to do.

* Let them know the special memories you have of their loved one. Another pastor, Burt Bunner, called me from another state several times just to see how I was doing and told me how he missed knowing my husband was praying for him. A year later he still checks on me to let me know he is praying for me.

* Do not hesitate to do anything that you think might be a blessing to someone who is hurting no matter how small. Do it! It may be the very thing that will help them through a difficult day.

* Be helpful to those who need your wisdom. Our lawyer and his secretary went out of their way to be of help and proved their friendship, which meant so much at a time when I needed it most. Lawyers are often represented unfairly; Tom and his staff were a friend to me as well as my lawyer.

* Do what your heart tells you to do, and do not be concerned if it is the right thing or not. Just showing you care means so much.

* Be a good neighbor. I will always be thankful for friends and neighbors like Marsha and Bruce Metz. Marsha, a nurse, not only became one of my dearest friends, but she was there constantly checking on me. I want to be that kind of friend.

* Just remember these things can be true for anyone who is going through any pain, not just a death. Everyone needs to know that someone cares and is there for them.

* A phone call saying, "I just want you to know I am thinking of you and if you need anything, day or night, I really want to be there."

* If family is out of town, offer to care for things they are unable to. When I was out of town with my children, our girls would send flowers for their dad's grave, and our friends Wayne and Tami Beverly would make sure they were placed on his grave

for us. What a blessing to be able to count on someone when we were away.

* No act of kindness goes unnoticed by those who are hurting.
* Friendships are cherished more at this time, and the pain is made lighter just knowing you care.
* Some things may be best unsaid, such as:

1. This was God's will (may cause them to blame God).
2. God knows what is best (and He does, but at this time it may not seem best to them).
3. Be thankful you still have other children. No one can take another's place in our hearts.
4. You will find good in this. (Right now it may not seem good.)
5. Do not tell them you know how they feel.
6. You will go on; life does. (Right now, there is a pause in their life.)
7. Time has a way of healing our hearts. (Their heart is broken.)
8. Remember—others have gone through this same thing and made it; you will too.

The best thing you can do is just be there for them. Your presence and love speak volumes that words can never say. If they begin to cry, let them cry. You do not need to say anything to help them. They are grieving. Grieving cannot be fixed; it needs healing, and that only comes with time.

13

How We Live Affects Others

When my husband suddenly passed from this life to a life with God, all I could think was, *What will I do without him?* I had been with him longer than I have been with anyone else here on earth. We had been together for most of our lives. I cried for several weeks, and one day I read in Romans 14:7, "For none of us liveth to himself, and no man dieth to himself." God spoke to my heart through these words that others are affected by how I live, how I act, and what I say and do.

My girls, my grandchildren, family, and friends are affected by my actions. If I allow them to see me give up and allow my grief to completely overtake me, I am showing them God is not enough and is not true to His word. What I say and do may cause another to serve God or turn away from Him. This is true in all of my life, in the good and the bad; what I say and do affects those around me.

In my loneliness and the empty place that is left in my everyday life, I know Paul is now living the victorious life he long anticipated. He is now in the actual presence of God. We can believe and know that for sure. How do I know that? The Bible tells me so. How I live does affect the life of others, not just when I am hurting but in all of life.

My girls and I had a funeral and buried the body of the man who loved us and gave his life in so many ways to take care of us, but his soul and spirit were already with the Lord. His funeral was for family and friends, not for him. Death cannot touch the soul, heart, and spirit that lives within us. The day he died, I can almost imagine the angels in heaven saying, "A saint of God is coming home," and our Lord Jesus greeting him with open arms and saying, "Welcome home, thou good and faithful servant."

The Bible tells us at the moment of death, we go immediately to be with the Lord. God's word is filled with His promises letting us know for sure our loved one is alive and with Him if he or she was a child of God. God makes this promise to those of us who are still alive. And because He makes this promise to me, I can face the future! Dear one reading this, you too can have this peace and assurance. Read what the Bible says and believe it.

I am convinced that all the sickness of this life, any pain, suffering, hardship, and all misunderstandings will be as nothing compared to the glory that awaits us. I find peace in knowing my husband no longer will have to face this old world and all its troubles and trials. As my daughter Renee' stated on the day her dad died, "My dad was too good for this old world, so God took him home." I am thankful we were allowed to live in the world we live in, but this world is not forever; it is only to prepare us for the one that will never end! No longer will my husband have to fall from weakness, bad knees, pain, bad heart, cancer, and so many other things. He can now enjoy being with God and those who have gone on before him. This has helped me to go on knowing the pain I now have is no longer his.

Even though we are never really prepared for the death of a loved one, we know that a brighter day is ahead for us who have accepted the Lord Jesus as our Lord and Savior. This world we are living in is not the end. There is going to be a new heaven and a new earth, which will never ever end. I am looking forward to that world when my life here on earth is over. If I truly believe this, even in the midst of my grief in missing my husband, I want others to see in me a source of faith and strength that only God gives when we are suffering. *I can say that God is there in everything we go through in life. He has not lost His power to heal our wounded heart and soul.*

A prayer we can pray is, "God, my heart is broken; I need Your love and strength to help me while it heals." He is doing that for me and will do that for anyone who puts their trust in Him. To those who are trusting in some other god, I feel sorry for them. My God lived, died, and rose again, and He is coming back for all who have put their trust in Him. They cannot say that!

Our pain will be used in a greater way than we can imagine right now. Because of what we go through in life, we learn lessons we never could have learned any other way. And we learn in a far greater way just how precious life and those around us are.

For many days, it seemed that all I could think about was what was missing in my life and what my husband's death took away from the life we had together. Then I began to think of what I still have because of him. I still have memories of the past when we were young, raising our children, many blessings, and happy times. His leaving did not take this away from me. I can still cherish the faith he had in God and his teachings, how he loved his family, who he was, and what he left with me in the lives of our children and grandchildren. Each time I talk to one of them, I can feel the love he had for them; I hear his voice when one of them says, "I miss Dad," or "When I do this, I think of Dad." A lot of who they are physically and spiritually is because of his faithfulness in teaching them to trust and love God.

My life and thinking were shaped in so many ways by my husband's example. I am spending more time thinking of what I have left because of him, and I am thankful for that. Yes, I have times when I still cry, but I understand a little more of what Job meant when he said, "My ears had heard of you before, but now my eyes have seen you." Through my tears, I have been able to see more clearly things I never saw before.

Healing begins to come when we can cherish what we have left. I will never be able to let go completely, nor do I want to. The legacy my husband has left behind will be part of my life forever.

14

Doctors Said Six Weeks; God Gave Him Fifteen Years

Even though my husband's health continued to fail after heart surgeries, eight heart attacks, thyroid disease, strokes, cancer, kidney disease, crippling arthritis, and more, he never stopped. We may say, "How could anyone live with so many health problems?" My answer is only by the grace of God, and no matter how good doctors may be, only God has that kind of power! I write this to say, "Never give up." Only God knows when we will take our last breath. The value of a person is not in what he or she can or cannot do, but who he or she is.

For almost forty years my husband preached, traveled worldwide on the mission field, and gave his all to tell others of the God who loved them and died for them. He never once asked anyone to help him financially, but he trusted God, and God never failed. We will never know until heaven how many men, women, and children are there because of his love and faithfulness.

After many heart attacks and ill health, he felt the time had come to pass the torch at First Baptist Church to his faithful and godly assistant, David Nutt. Paul became a member and began to sit in the pew while another man became pastor of the church he had served for almost forty years. Every time we would leave church, he would say to me, "Brother Dave gave a good message. I learned a lot today." He always found good in others. Another lesson I learned from him was this: *"When your life changes and you can no longer do what you once did, encourage others to pick up the torch and run with it."* He did that! He felt it was time for Pastor Nutt to lead, and Paul did all he could to support and encourage him, and he looked out for him.

The doctors had told him to get his life in order as six weeks or months would be a long life for him. Little did they know his life was already in order spiritually, and now all he had to do was to finish whatever work he had to do here on earth. He was ready to go when God said, "Come home." Isn't that a wonderful way to live? In spite of all this, he continued to preach when he was able, and he continued to increase in his prayer ministry. He would still get up long before dawn and pray for pastors, missionaries, our family, lost souls, friends, and for God's work on earth to increase. He spent hours and hours in God's word and seeking God.

In Second Corinthians 4:16 we read: "For which cause we faint not; but though our outward man perish, yet the inner man is renewed day by day." I saw that happening in my husband for years as his earthly body became weaker and weaker, yet the inner man became stronger spiritually. He enjoyed every moment he had with God, our family, and friends, and I saw a God-like spirit of quietness, humbleness, and peace in him like I saw in very few Christians. One of the main things I saw was answered prayers in the lives of others he prayed for that perhaps never knew he was praying for them. Many times, when we heard good news about someone, or saw answered prayer in the lives of others or our family, I knew he had been praying for them and God answered.

In my writing, I am not trying to elevate my husband as a sinless and perfect man; at best, he was man. He had his faults, and he and I both knew that, and he would be the first to admit it! He was not perfect, but he was the one God had in my life that was who I needed. But to the best of my ability, I will try to write what I know God can do when someone puts their faith and trust in God and how there is help when you are going through the worst time in your life, no matter what that may be. I can write about this because I saw it in my husband. People need to know this more today than ever before. So many do not know the God he knew and who lives today for all of us. My husband felt that far too many have made too much of man and admired them more than giving the honor that was due God.

On November 28, 2015, one day after his seventy-third birthday, God called him home. There was no sad farewell, no grieving (on his part), no struggle, just a word to our daughter Renee': "I can't breathe." Then, he was gone from this world to his new home with God, breathing that heavenly air.

My heart grieves for those who have to watch a loved one linger with a long sickness and suffering. Even though he had numerous health problems, he never complained. He kept going to church, traveling to see the family, and eating out; he just would not stop. In fact, I got so used to him just being him that I had begun to think we still had a long life ahead together. Whether it is easier on those of us who have a loved one leave suddenly, or to watch one linger on in their sickness, I do not know. But I do know this: the pain of loss is like no other pain, and I never knew what others went through until their pain became mine.

I know what God can and will do to comfort us in our deepest pain. He is watching over us, and many times He brought us through things we never would have been able to handle had He not been there giving us strength we did not have. Only God could do that!

How long will our pain continue? No one can put a time on our heart. Our life changed the day our loved one died, and our life will never be the same again. There will always be that "missing link," but we can and will adjust to the life we now have. Easy—no! When a loved one dies or a drastic change happens, our whole life changes and life will never be as it was before. Before Paul died, I was a wife and we were a couple, but now everything we did together, I do alone. Even when I am with my children, we all sense that missing part of our family. Where once it was *we,* it is now *me.*

15

We're Here and It's Now

One second my husband was here; the next second, he was gone. That is how quickly life happens and changes. We do not realize how short time here on this earth is when we are busy living it. Then, when we see death or sickness in the face, the first thing we feel is shock, sadness, and grief, a feeling of sudden emptiness inside, and as we walk away from our loved one, it begins to sink in—*they are gone*! The body may still be there for us to look at and touch, but we know the spirit, the heart, and the soul of that one is gone. Where is the one that loved us, cared for us, the heart that felt life; where are they now?

We may not understand everything, but I hope as I share my thoughts and what I know for sure is true, it will help others who are grieving to see God is true to His promise never to leave or forsake us. No matter what anyone may be going through, He is there. Not only is He there, but He is almighty and can do for us what no one or anything else in this world can do.

Once we have faced death and we see how quickly life changes, we begin to realize and value life like we never have before. It is so important that we cherish the moment with those around us. We begin to have a new feeling about life, realizing like never before that it is not things but people that are important. Without them, no matter what we have, nothing in this world can take their place. I have talked to many critically ill people, and never once did I hear them say, "I wish I had worked harder, bought that new car, had a bigger house, or went on that big vacation." No, but I have heard them say, "I wish I had lived my life differently, told my family I loved them more often, spent more time with them, and not been so concerned about other things that now mean absolutely nothing." My husband always said he and I had riches that no amount of money could buy.

It is so important that we take time to look at the real values of life—God and our family—because we never know when life may change. Tell those you love now, say I am sorry now, and tell them what they mean to you now. Forgive now, and encourage your loved ones now. Make time for them now, and thank them now for being who they are to you. Now is all we have, and once a loved one is gone, you will never have that time again. Right now, is the time to enjoy every moment you can with those you love most. After they are gone, you will wish you had! We live *here* right now, but this is not the final place. Our final place, when we know Jesus, is where there is no sickness, no death, a new heaven, and a new earth; but until that time comes, *now* is all we have.

When a loved one dies, a part of us dies also. I remember leaving the hospital and feeling an emptiness within me I had never felt before. My first thought was, *What will I do now?* I never knew until that moment, and as days went by, how much I looked to and depended on Paul. He was my husband and my best friend in the good and bad of life. He was always there for me. Even if he was in the hospital, he was still there with me, and I could visit him and talk to him on the phone and seek his advice, but not now. He always said to me in hard times, "Look to God, and take one day at a time." God gave me a scripture from the very beginning. It was Isaiah 42:16: "I (God) will bring the blind by a way that they know not (that was me) I will lead them in paths that they have not known (that was ahead for me now) I will make darkness light before them and crooked things straight. These things will I do unto them and not forsake them."

That was His promise to me. A peace came to my heart, and I knew God was going to lead me and take care of me in all my fears and uncertainties in whatever was ahead for me. It was now time, like never before, to do what my husband always taught us to do: *trust God*! God would lead me and my girls in the way we should go. All I had to do was wait on the Lord and listen and obey His leading. He will also do that for those of you who may be reading this. I can tell you that I have had wisdom to do some things I never had to do before or knew how to do. God has been faithful, and when I have needed wisdom, God has either sent someone to help me, or I just knew what to do. People can say what they will, but I say, "We can trust God to do for us what we cannot do ourselves."

If you are reading this and have never accepted Jesus as your Lord and Savior, now is certainly the time to do so. Many have said to me, "I never called on Him before, and I don't feel right doing it now." Do not let the evil one put this in your mind.

John 3:16–18 tells us, "For God so loved the world that He gave His only begotten Son, that whosoever believeth in him should not perish but have everlasting life. For God sent not his Son into the world to condemn the world; but that the world through him might be saved. He that believeth on him is not condemned; but he that believeth not is condemned already, because he hath not believed in the name of the only begotten Son of God."

God wants to come into our pain, and when we feel we cannot go another day in whatever has caused our pain, He is there. Pain of any kind is hard, but never too hard for God to come into and heal us. Whatever has caused your pain, your life has changed, and the way you will live now will be different than before. We need to make the best of the life we have now because now is all we have. We never know what tomorrow or the next moment may bring into our life.

Everyone has pain and suffering—-failed marriages, sickness, death, lost jobs and security, and heartaches of all kinds. You may feel your whole life has been turned upside down, and you wonder if you will ever be able to put it all back together again. God can do what you or no one else can do. He can restore you to a life that only He alone can remake.

Sooner or later, life brings to everyone heartache and pain, but God can fill that void. He can and will give the comfort and healing to that open wound. God knows, and He is with us in our deepest pain.

16

Getting through the Hard Days

Many have told me how hard holidays, birthdays, the day a loved one passed away, and family celebrations can be when you have lost someone you love. We were just going into the Christmas season when Paul passed away, and I dreaded Christmas. Yet, the Christ of Christmas was all He promised He would be. Tears flowed as we missed the presence of our loved one. The hardest thing for me was remembering how he loved Christmas and having all the family together. They were his greatest gifts here on earth. He did not need anything materially. I realized all the good memories we had would always be with us, and because of that, his presence would be in our hearts forever.

Our oldest daughter Renee' gave each of us a gold star with the date to hang on our tree. She gave it to us to symbolize the significance of Daniel 12:3: "And they that be wise shall shine as the brightness of the firmament; and they that turn many to righteousness as the stars for ever and ever." Not only was it special then, but each of us kept it up all year next to his picture. And each year I am sure that it will hang in a special place on each of our Christmas trees.

Our daughter Lynn wrote a tribute to her dad and put it in all her Christmas cards:

A Tribute to My Dad

My dad will be spending Christmas in heaven with Jesus this year. Our hearts are hurting so deeply as we miss his smile, his wisdom, and his love. We just miss everything about him. He was so understanding, so patient, so loving, and so Christlike. My dad never asked for anything! He was content every day of his life. He always focused on the true meaning of Christmas—and the true meaning of life. I never heard my dad complain—and I cannot recall one cruel word he ever said about anyone, anywhere.

Dad truly will have the best Christmas ever! Ours will be very different. Our Christmas will be filled with tears, wonderful memories, and gratitude for a dad who led our family with dignity and as much love as a man possibly could. He leaves behind a legacy that is second to none. We are all challenged to live the way Dad did, putting Christ first and making sure that everyone who comes in contact with us sees Jesus in our lives.

Dad, thank you for taking the time to make sure that your whole family would all be together again. Because of your influence and your prayers, we are all coming to join you in heaven. I love you, Daddy! We will spend Christmas together again.

Dr. Paul R. Knierim

November 27, 1942–November 28, 2015

To see more about my dad's life and a video, please visit www.Leavittfuneralhome.com, Belpre, Ohio. It is listed under Reverend Paul R. Knierim.

Father's Day

Our daughter Renee' wanted to do something special to honor her dad on Father's Day. She had a special card made celebrating his life and sent it to family members and friends. Her dad had a burden that everyone he came in contact with would hear about the Lord he loved, especially his family. She also included with the picture card the following letter:

Dear Family:

This will be my first Father's Day without my dad, Paul R. Knierim. Dad went home to heaven this year. Words could never express how much our entire family misses him. He was the kindest, most caring, and most loving father anyone could ever have. He lived his life for God and others.

Over the last few months, I have been thinking of a way to honor my dad's memory for this Father's Day. I thought of all of you—the Herman and Knierim families that he loved so dearly. Although miles and years have a way of separating us, I want to let you know that my dad spoke of you all so often. He loved you and prayed for your families. As a girl, I loved hearing stories of Uncle John and Aunt Alice, and Uncle Bill and Aunt Marjorie. Dad would often talk about his cousins: Mary Ann, Lexie, Jennifer, Bill, Nancy, and John. He was so happy when he would hear of your accomplishments. Thank you for all that you meant to him.

How my dad loved my grandparents and Aunt Kathy and Uncle Tom. Many times, we would get out the old slide projector and watch slides of Dad's and Aunt Kathy's growing up years. He had so much joy telling us the stories of their family. He was so thankful God gave him such a special family. Enclosed is a copy of a photograph that

Dad always kept on his dresser. I want to thank my Aunt Kathy for the love and support she has been to us this year. She has cried with us and has taken time to talk about the many fond memories of Dad we share. She has been there every step of the way. We love you so much, Aunt Kathy.

I will see my dad again one day because of the gift of salvation and the blessed hope of heaven. He was ready to meet the Lord, and that is the greatest gift he could have left our family. His greatest desire was to tell every one of his Lord and Savior.

"For God so loved the world He gave His only Son, that whosoever believeth in Him should not perish but have everlasting life" (John 3:16).

Renee' (Knierim) Gamble

Our daughter Rachel helps our grandson Michael, who makes boxes for needy kids through the Samaritan Ministry. I know she has chosen a name from the angel tree for Christmas and sees that a child will have some special gifts that he or she might not normally get. She also helps others in various ways. Her dad was one to give to missions and those less fortunate, and our Rachel is one of the most giving people I know. So is like her dad in this respect.

These are just a few things our girls did to include the memory of their dad on special days. Even though we may be with others at these special times, there is still that empty chair, missing laughter, and an empty space in our hearts. The special days are hard, and it is all right to cry because love never dies with our loved one; love lives on forever. I have a more tender and understanding heart for those who are walking the same path we are now walking. My heart goes out to them like never before.

On the one-year anniversary of my husband's birthday, our daughter Lynn had a special card made with a picture of her dad and a special memorial to honor him. She sent it as a thank you to many who had prayed for us and sent notes during the year. She also put a memorial in the local newspaper.

Dr. Paul R. Knierim
Promoted to Heaven Nov. 28, 2015

Another way to keep alive the life of one who is gone is by making a life or memory book. One of the reasons I am writing about who my husband was is to keep his memory alive and preserved for generations to come, not only for my children and grandchildren, but for others who may be reading this many years from now. He may be gone, but his memory will stay with us forever. Also, I wanted it to be a help to others who are hurting and to share with them ways to keep alive memories of their loved ones.

I thought of you with love today,
But that is nothing new.
I thought about you yesterday,
And days before that too.
I think of you in silence.
I often speak your name.
All I have are memories
And your picture in a frame.
Your memory is my keepsake,
With which I'll never part.
He has you in His keeping;
I have you in my heart.

—Author unknown

Our tears show our love for those who are away from us, not our weakness. Life changes so rapidly; it may be someday, or years from now, someone will pick up this book and find peace in his or her deepest pain from the scriptures and from the life of an old preacher who believed, trusted, and saw what God could and would do for those who put their faith in Him. Our world and its absolutes may change, but God never changes!

17

A Peaceful Heart

A peaceful heart—this is a wonderful statement, but one that is sometimes hard to live by. I certainly am not one who is a good example of someone who always has faith and never worries. But this I do know: "I know that I can trust God and can be secure in the place I am in today." He knows what is inside of me, my thoughts and my fears, and He is as close to me as the very breath I take. He knows my heart's desire is to trust Him completely in all of life. I know I can trust Him because He has proven faithful in the past. I find peace and comfort in knowing He knows and sees what lies ahead for me, even though I cannot see it. He is helping me to rebuild my life without Paul. There is so much help and encouragement in the Bible. To some reading this, they may think this is a crutch, but to me it has been a lifeline!

When I look back now at the many times I found Paul alone praying and reading his Bible, I wish I had just quietly gone in and just sat in the same room instead of trying not to disturb him. One just knew the presence of God was in that room. He truly was ready to give his life to honor and serve the Lord Jesus Christ. This can only be lived when one is so deep in commitment to God and their desire is to live and serve Him with their whole being. Nothing or no one could shake his faith. He had burdens and trials like everyone does, and his burdens were hard to bear, but he never wavered in his faith and trust in God. His life exemplified Isaiah 32:17: "And the work of righteousness shall be peace; and the effect of righteousness quietness and assurance forever."

We always enjoyed being together as a family. We were not a "super religious" family by any means, and we failed in so many ways like all families do. But when God called him home, we all said, "What will we do without Dad praying for us?" I truly believe he still is praying for us like never before, but wouldn't it be wonderful if we all could leave this legacy to our children? Nothing we could leave of material value could compare with this treasure. Our children will always be able to say, "Our dad prayed for us!"

When life takes a piece of your heart, we all need something to hold on to. To me this was the wonderful Lord Jesus and His word. Down through the ages of time, people of every walk of life have died and faced many heartaches. Small children die, young people die, good people die, and people who are evil die. Our life here is not the end, but because of Calvary, when we put our faith in Jesus, the One who died for us, and rose again, we will find peace now and will live forever in the new heaven and the new earth.

If I were to be asked what book or author was used to change my life, it would be God and the Bible, and I am not trying to be spiritual in saying this. We often look for a book that will help us, but if that book does not point us to the one true book, no matter who the author is, we will never find the peace we are longing for. God's book, like no other, is inspired by God, the one true and only God. No author can do what God can do in us. The Bible is God's message to us today leading us to life everlasting in Jesus and peace here on earth.

I know this can make a difference in a person's life because my husband lived this way, and I witnessed in him a peace and joy that I must admit far too often was not in me. Many times, we let the stresses of life rob us of this peace. Even though his life had unbelievable health problems and his physical body was fading away, his spiritual body was being renewed daily.

The truth is that I wrote much of this with tears of sorrow, pain, and heartache, and it was after my husband was gone that I realized like never before how blessed I had been to have been married to such a man. I am afraid that all too often I took for granted or just got used to what was before me. Do not neglect or take lightly those God has put around you. We get so busy living with them as family, and sometimes we fail to see just who God has put in our midst.

I thank God that my husband was the man he was, and even though we all knew how much he loved us, we knew (and now more than ever) how much he was willing to give of himself to prayer and Bible study, so that our family would not only know how to live while he was here with us but also after he was gone. Our Lord Jesus did this far greater than anyone ever has, and His teachings have left with us His word on how to find His peace in the times of pain and struggles of life.

My husband wrote this chorus when he was away on a mission trip:

More Time for Prayer

More time for prayer
Yes, more time for prayer;
you can show that you care,
and give more time to prayer.

He truly was a man of prayer, and I saw through his life what prayer and faith can do. So often we use prayer as a last resort, but he taught me that prayer should be our first and only resort at all times. He told me many times that prayer was not begging but believing, and he believed that when he prayed, God would answer his prayer in the best way and he could trust God for His answer. *He did not just pray and hope it would happen; he just waited for it to happen.*

I often felt his faith was like that of a little child. When our kids were small and would be fearful of thunder and lighting and other fears, he would go into their room and tell them about Jesus and how He was watching over them, and he would pray with them. At nights when Renee' was small, I could hear her say, "Jesus up in heaven looking down in my room," and soon she was sound asleep. Because she could believe her father and what he told her, she could trust him and rest in knowing that Jesus was watching over her, and as a child, she could say such a little prayer and go right off to sleep. Many times, I would lay awake with the burdens of tomorrow on my mind while she would be sound asleep with no fears because she knew God was watching over her. I believe that was what Jesus was teaching us in Mark 10:15 when He used a child to teach us: "Verily I say unto you, Whosoever shall not receive the kingdom of God as a little child, he shall not enter therein." That is what faith is. When our girls' dad told them that Jesus was watching over them, that was all they needed. Why can we not trust our Father God like that? He tells us in Matthew 17:20 that if you and I would have just enough faith as a "grain" of a mustard seed what our faith could do. Jesus is up in heaven watching over us, and we can trust Him.

My husband had learned how to leave all to God's care—his life, his health, his peace, and all that concerned him. He could trust God for the present and the future.

18

Preparing to Die

Over the years I watched my husband change from a man who often, in his zeal to honor and serve Christ, came across to some as one who was very strong and uncompromising in his preaching, to one who still spoke the same truths, but with a sweet, humble spirit of love. Even though in earlier years he loved just as deeply, the years of walking with the Lord had given him an even more loving and understanding heart.

He was known as a preacher who strongly stood on his beliefs and what God's word said, no matter how it hurt him, how others would see him, accuse him, or walk away from him. You do not hear of too many like that today. Some did not understand when he refused to compromise and go along with them, but he stayed true to what he believed God wanted him to do, and they knew it.

I also saw a man who was blessed by God more and more as he stayed faithful to Him and His calling. He was a servant, and he was faithful in his prayer life; his living the undying truths of God taught me God is faithful and never fails to be with us, bless us, and give us grace to follow Him when we obey and trust Him. He taught us that it was important that we knew Jesus personally, not just what we knew about Him.

Early in our ministry he was up before dawn praying, and many times late at night I would find him alone on his knees talking with God. On Sundays, and anytime there were services at church, or before he was to preach, he was at the church alone hours before services began praying for God's power and His will to be done in the service. Others did not see or know this, but the girls and I did. When there were problems, people fighting against him and causing problems in the church, financial burdens, he never discussed this with us; he always went to God about any issue that came up, and when he felt he knew what God wanted him to do and say, he did it. When he felt it was God's leading for his assistant pastor to become the pastor, the church was completely out of debt and all the buildings stood as a witness to the faithfulness of God and His provision.

Years ago, our daughter Lynn composed a song entitled "Early in the Morning" because of what she saw in the prayer life of her dad. At the top of the music she had these words printed: *To my dad with love. Thank you for your godly example and for the many times I saw you "early in the morning" on your knees.*

It was early in the morning that Jesus Christ arose
And now He lives in heaven as we now know
The grave was opened wide, and it was plain to see
That once for all there was for man, a way to victory!

Early in the morning, the wondrous work was done
Early in the morning, they greeted God's Glorious Son!
It was early in the morning, the wondrous work was done.

It is early in the morning that we are called to pray
To seek the face of God and strength for each new day.
As we read in God's Word and seek His blessed face,
Once again delight is found in His sufficient grace!

What if early in the morning, our Saviour comes again
Oh, will you be found ready, when He desends?
He shall come in the twinkling of an eye
Early in the morning, we may reach the eastern sky!

Words Pastor Paul R. Knierim Music and arrangement Lynn Knierim

God blessed our family, our church, and our lives, and even though there were many valleys, it seemed we always made it to the mountaintop in due time. I praise God for that and for a man who was willing to do it God's way. I did not always see this at the time, and often worried—yes worried— but he had a faith that no matter what was happening, he trusted God.

I often felt he was not appreciated for the man he was. That was never important to him. In fact, he felt the higher up you went in the eyes of men, the more apt one was to become prideful and self-centered and become more interested in keeping that influence with people than one was to God. He always said we had more to lose when people praised us than we had to gain when we sought to please God, and it was far better to have God's approval than man's approval. He never longed for anything for himself but gave—oh, did he give—to missions, the church, and the work of God. Colossians 3:1–3 says, "If ye then be risen with Christ, seek those things which are above, where Christ sitteth on the right hand of God. Set your affections on things above and not on things on the earth. For ye are dead and your life is hid in Christ with God." He truly set his mind and heart on things above and not on the things of this earth. Many times, in my flesh, I wanted to tell people all he did, but he never wanted that, and I have honored his wishes.

I never saw pride in him. I am sure it must have raised its ugly head at times because the devil never gives up on any of us. He often told me pride had caused many a man of God to become proud of his accomplishments and to become more concerned of what others thought of him rather than what God thought. He never wanted to fall into that category. In all his years of ministry, most people never knew he had several earned and honorary degrees.

Often, we talk about "great men of old" who were great saints of faith, and we fail to realize there are some who are alive today who God places in our midst. My husband was one of these men! Often when someone dies, we make him or her a saint. I am not trying to do that and would be afraid to do so, as I said before; he had faults like all humans do. I am just stating that there was a man who truly walked with God in my midst. Perfect—no! Human faults—yes! There may be people in your life who are like that. If so, thank God for them and pray for them. We look at what we think is success and are apt to admire one who we think is great, when walking among us may be one who truly walks with God, perhaps with a quiet and humble spirit.

God has placed some very godly people in our world, and if ever there is a time it is needed, it is now, and perhaps it is not until they die that we recognize it. They may not be who we think they are. They may not have been well known, but millions may have been saved because of their faithfulness in praying. We will never know how many came to a saving knowledge of Christ because of their prayers. They may have been someone who gave their life to praying for those who all over the world are working in God's vineyard. In his later years, my husband could not do a lot of things he used to do because of his health, but he felt he could pray for those who were doing the work of God, and when he heard great things were happening in their lives, he was always happy for them. He prayed for revival and for pastors all over the world and for their ministry.

During his ministry, he traveled and preached on mission fields to the Philippines, Greece, Austria, Germany, Hungary, Israel, Italy, India, Peru, Belize, Spain, England, Mexico, Romania, Portugal, Switzerland, Ireland, Rome, and perhaps some that I have forgotten. We will never know how many lives were changed because of his burden to travel around the world to tell others how they could go to heaven and not to hell. I have no idea how many people all over the world are saved and are either in heaven or on their way to heaven because of his burden to reach everyone everywhere.

In looking through his files, I found this in his computer:

This Is Your Future

Everyone wonders what the future will hold for them. In this area, there is much uncertainty. However, in one aspect there is **ABSOLUTE CERTAINTY** concerning our future. **EVERYONE** will spend all of eternity in either Heaven or Hell. There is no exception to this fact. Heaven is wonderful beyond our fondest imaginations and hell is horrible beyond our worst nightmares. You will live in conscious bliss or conscious torment forever. You decide which place will be your eternal home. In order to go to hell, simply live however you wish and do whatever you want. Your eternal punishment will be banishment from God's love and presence forever. You reject God's love and commandments in this life and He will reject you forever.

However, YOU CAN SPEND ETERNITY IN HEAVEN! The Bible tells us to REPENT (Luke 13: 3&5) and BELIEVE (Acts 16:31; John 3:16-18,36). God's gift of eternal life (Eph. 2:8-9) is available to ANYONE who will meet God's conditions of repentance (choosing to serve God and no longer self) and faith (trust in Jesus Christ and His payment on the cross for your sins).

In Joshua 24:15, we read that Joshua challenged Israel to *"Choose you this day whom ye will serve..."* (either false gods or the true God). Everyone must make that same decision. Choose God, and heaven will be your eternal home. Reject God, and His command to repent and believe, and Hell will be your eternal home.

19

This World Is Not Our Home

Matthew 24:35 tells us that this old world will pass away, but God's word will never pass away. Most of us push death far back in our minds until we have to deal with it. Death is a word none of us want to think about when it comes to one of our loved ones. It is a part of life we take for granted until we are forced to look it in the face. We have connected it with the word *final*. My husband truly handled this with dignity and grace like no one I knew, certainly not me. I, like others, had pushed it to the back of my mind until one day I came face-to-face with death and how quickly life can change.

Our Lord faced death without fear, and He talked about it often with his disciples. Paul did with me. The more my husband became detached from this old world (his hope was planted in the eternal life waiting him), the more he actually enjoyed his life here. He knew this life here would someday end, but the life awaiting him was forever. He could not see (as our Lord did) all that was ahead for him, but from all he read in God's word, he believed and had faith it was real. He found the secret of living life here and looking forward to the life that God promised in His word. That very life is available to all of us and to our loved ones. Just knowing this and believing it helps in our pain. He knew God was in control, whether it was what was going on in our world or our personal life. He did not worry or fear the unknown;

nothing he had to face was stronger than God. He had known and experienced the power of God, and he totally trusted that.

Often, he would just sit in his chair with his eyes closed, and I would say, "Are you sleeping?" He would answer, "No, just enjoying the presence of God." He was still in his heart and soul and knew no matter what, God was God and that was enough for whatever was going on in our life. He trusted and rested in the Lord. Psalm 48:14 says, "For this God is our God forever and forever; He will be our guide even unto death."

That kind of faith made my husband enjoy life here, his family, and all the blessings of God in a greater way because he knew he was just passing through this life. He wanted to do all he could for everyone he could, especially the Lord. He was free to be who he was, and he accepted others for who they were—imperfect, yes, but someday all that imperfection in him and others would be made perfect in the new life to come.

For those who may doubt there is going to be a new heaven and a new earth, God's word says in Revelation 21:1: "And I saw a new heaven and a new earth: for the first heaven and the first earth were passed away; and there was no more sea." This may sound like some kind of teaching "out of this world." *It is!* There is a new world ahead for all those who die in Christ, and I can prove it. John 14:1–3 says, "Let not your heart be troubled: ye believe in God, believe also in me. In my Father's house are many mansions: if it were not so I would have told you. I go to prepare a place for you and if I go and prepare a place for you I will come again and receive you unto myself; that where I am, there ye may be also." First Corinthians 2:9–10 says, "But as it is written eye hath not seen, nor ear heard, neither have entered into the heart of man, the things which God hath prepared for them that love Him. But God hath revealed them unto us by the Spirit, for the Spirit searcheth all things, yea, the deep things of God."

My husband believed and taught there was a heaven waiting for those who have trusted Christ as their Savior and a hell waiting for those who do not believe and put their trust in the shed blood of Jesus. For those who have accepted Christ, their spirit goes immediately to be with

God, and those who have rejected Jesus will go to a place of torments with Satan. Both are eternal and forever. Oh, I pray, dear one, you will be in the first group. When we die, there is a life hereafter. Please do not neglect that truth.

My desire in writing the things I have is to help those who are grieving who may think death is the end of life for our loved one, or that the trouble and heartaches we are going through will never get better. Just listen to what Jesus said in John 11:25, "Jesus said: I am the resurrection. and the life. He that believeth in me. though he were dead. yet shall he live." My husband was convinced that when Christians die, their spirit goes immediately to be with the Lord. I believe he is experiencing that right now! I do not think anyone can really know all that is prepared and waiting for us when we die. I do know this: none of us know the moment we will take our last breath here on earth, but we can know that when we do, there is a new life waiting for us.

Our loved one may be gone away from us, but the life and influence here still live on. Do not be afraid to remember and cherish the things his or her life left behind; share those things with others.

We never know what tomorrow may bring. As I am writing this, a special news broadcast came over the air that a gunman fired shots on several of our GOP representatives who were on a ball field practicing for a charity game to help others. One of our congressmen is in critical condition and four others wounded. I am sure neither they nor their families thought something like this would happen when their loved one left home this morning. God has promised to be with us in the worst pain of our life, and the shock of this certainly has to be one of the worst pains ever for those families whose hearts are broken and confused right now. I know this: there is someone who is with our country and these families throughout these dark times.

Paul was used in my life to teach me so much about God, and God is using his death to teach me to have a deeper compassion and love for those who are suffering. I have also learned to cherish the moment now. I certainly do not know all that is going on in the pain of those who are suffering right now, but I know how deep pain feels, and I can pray for those that suffer.

20

New Beginnings

Change is hard, and when what you have been used to is no longer possible, you must learn to make a new life. Now comes the task of going through the life Paul and I had built together. What once was needed for a family, and then just the two of us, has now been reduced to just one person—me!

Going through my husband's personal belongings and the things from our home of almost fifty years is not something that can be done in a week. For instance, in his study he had so many books and probably a hundred or more old Bibles and testaments. He could never stand to see a Bible in a bargain store sold for a quarter or on clearance, so he would buy it and put in on his shelf, in addition to all the Bibles he used and wore out over the years. One just does not discard a Bible. So, after everyone had taken what they wanted, and I had given many of his Bibles away to family and friends, we still had over seven boxes of Bibles to donate to mission work and outreach ministries for those who may not have a Bible. I also had to go through his clothing, personal items, and things that had special memories only to the two of us. This was hard to do. To me the key was just taking my time and deciding what I felt I could do without, finding what the girls would want and could use, and then sharing with others some of his earthly possessions.

Finally, a decision had to be made to let go of many things, and once the decision was made, I had to go on.

When facing new beginnings in life, consider Matthew 6:34: "Take therefore no thought for the morrow: for the morrow shall take thought for the things of itself. Sufficient unto the day is the evil thereof." Ask God what you are to do next. No one knows our future except God. We can trust Him to lead us into this time of change in our life. As I trust Him for today, He will give me the strength and leading for tomorrow when it comes. Proverbs 3:5–6 says, "Trust in the Lord with all thine heart; and lean not unto thy own understanding. In all thy ways acknowledge him, and he shall direct thy paths."

Four words that helped me were in Genesis 45:20: "regard not your stuff." That is what material things are—stuff! You cannot wrap your arms around the nicest furniture in the world and feel loved, only around your loved ones. Material things without love are just that— things! They cannot bring happiness. At the end of the day when you can look in the eyes of those you love and say, "I love you," that gives a peace and happiness that nothing else in this world can. All the money in the world cannot buy love. So, to me the most important thing is to be with those I love whenever I can because we only have this moment, and we need to cherish every second of it. Many have learned too late that the most precious valuables we have here on earth are our loved ones. Take good care of them.

Your pain may be a parent who is still here, but Alzheimer's has taken from them the memory of you; you are left with what to do, and you must now make decisions for them. You may feel uncomfortable going through their stuff and taking over for them the things that were private to them. This is hard, but remember that God is with you. *He is not just letting it happen; He is with us while it is happening.* It may seem our life may be out of control, but God never is. One of the things I try to do is not look back. If I do, it is hard to walk forward and go on. My daughter Renee' sent me a text with the words: "Don't look back; you are not going that way." Life changes for us, and we must make the most of where we are. My husband always felt the world sees our faith in God not by what happens to us but how we react to what happens.

Each morning when we awaken, we will experience a new beginning. We go through the day as we usually do until something happens that completely changes our whole life. It may be a serious accident, health problems, divorce, death, a wedding, a new birth, happy times, or sad times, but our life has changed that day from the normal. It is easy to adjust to the good things that happen, but we also have to face the not-so-good things. We find as we live life, changes do come, and when we have come through these changes, we find, no matter how hard the change was, perhaps many blessings came about because of that pain. We become a different person and hopefully a better person.

We never know if this will be the last time we will be able to share a day with someone we love. We think there is tomorrow to say and do what we did not have time to do today. Since we are not promised tomorrow, for ourselves or for those we love, we need to take the time now to let them know what they mean to us. If in our pain we learn to live today without regrets, then our pain has not been in vain. If someone has touched your life, tell him or her now. We are who we are today because of what we have gone through. Because of our pain, we can learn to love deeper than ever before.

For years my husband prayed for a young man by the name of Danny Gandee. He would visit him, pray for him, and not give up on him. One day Danny accepted Jesus as his Lord and Savior. Whenever he saw me or my husband, he would always express how thankful he was that Paul never gave up on him. Someday, he and Danny will be in heaven together. We need to pray for our friends and loved ones who do not know Christ and never give up on them. If someone has blessed your life, be like Danny and tell them. Do not wait until it is too late and then be sorry for what you wish you had done and said.

Each day, I now wake with the desire and prayer that God will open my eyes to know who I can encourage and help in the dark days of their life. My husband once made a statement when someone asked him, "Pastor, I need help, but I can't see God!" His reply was, "But God sees you and can help" (Psalm 46:1). He told that person that we do not need to see something to be helped and affected by it. The human eye cannot see the wind, but we still feel its presence and see what it can do. We cannot see God when we pray, but He sees our hearts and souls and can do what no one else can do.

Do not ever give up praying for someone and for God to work in the hearts and lives of others. The more we know God through prayer and His word, the more our faith will grow and the more peace we will have in our hearts and souls.

21

Unfulfilled Dreams—Making New Ones

We all know that dying is part of living, but not until we must face the death of someone close to us does it become a reality. We may long for someone to share our grief, and family and friends may try to help us, but it is a journey we each must go through alone. We all have unfulfilled dreams and regrets. Whether good or bad, my husband and I shared everything in life together. That alone is something to be grateful for. Many do not have those memories and have to live with broken homes and marriages. I never had to have that pain, and my heart grieves for those who are going through this heartache.

Our devotion to one another was one that only death could separate. It was not perfect by any means, but it was a commitment to one another "till death do us part." When one of us suffered, the other did also; we could see and feel it on each other's faces. When one was happy, the other was happy. Many today never get to know this because they walk away from what could have been a beautiful life together when problems come. We were different in so many ways. He was more quiet and serious, and I am more outgoing and full of fun. He taught me to take my life with God more serious, and I will always be thankful for that. I needed his godly influence in my life, and he needed me to help him see the silly and fun things of life—at least I hope so! I thank God that when problems came, we (by God's grace) saw it through together, and in our later years, we often said, "We have had a good life together," and we did!

till death do us part

We had planned to move down South, which would put us close to all three of our girls. We were going to be with them for the winter and then go back to Ohio and clear out the house there and say good-bye to friends. But one month before we were to leave, the Lord took Paul home. Our dream of moving to be near our girls never materialized. I no longer have the plans we had, but I am now facing the future ahead of me as to what is. We are not in charge of our life; God is. There will come a time in all our lives when we will be in a different place than we thought. What will we do? I know I cannot live with "what if"; I must go on from where I am now. Paul would want me to do that. Even though memories of what once was often tugs at my heart, I must live the life that is mine now. But this I know: God is with me.

Paul's life here on earth and his death showed the way for the girls and me to follow. We may make great plans for our marriage, the birth of our children, their college, and all of these things yet fail to make plans for the hereafter. My husband was prepared for death, and he left with us expressions of his love for God and his family by living the life he did before us. He left a memory to guide us to the next step in our life—going to be with the Lord. Jesus not only detached Himself from the things of earth but attached Himself fully to His Father's will. I saw that in my husband in his later years.

So the dreams Paul and I had together (other than being together in heaven) will no longer be here on this earth. I must now make new dreams with our children and everyone I meet. Death lurks in everyone's mind from time to time, but often we push it back, choosing not to think about it. When I think of Paul suddenly dying, that is not true. None of us die all at once. Every day we are closer to death. I knew my husband was ill, but I had seen God bring him through so much that I was fooled into believing that his death would not be for a long time to come, or that I may go first. That is exactly what most of us do; we push these thoughts into the back of our minds. Many today are living in the moment and fail to realize that moment is going to end. I cannot live "our dreams" anymore, but I can do all I can to honor the dreams we had and to live my life to honor the God we both loved and served, and try to honor my husband by doing what he would have done if he were here.

Until I had your pain, I did not realize how you hurt. I believe that is what God did when He gave His only Son to die for me. I believe that is what Jesus did for me on the cross and is doing right now. He feels my pain, and He alone is giving me strength I could never have within myself. I believe He felt my pain when He was on the cross and carrying the heavy burden of my sins, giving His life for mine, and feeling for me all that would lie ahead for me. Because of the pain He suffered for me, how could I ever doubt that right now He knows how I feel and how every person who is suffering feels. He went through death and the worst of pain for us so that we might have life.

My words are so hollow, so incomplete, but I am so thankful Jesus was willing to give His life for all so that we can find in Him all we need for now and forever. My life may have changed, but the One within me is still in control. I may change and my world may change, but God is the same yesterday, today, and forever. God has not died or lost His power or His love for us. He is with us in any trial we may have to go through.

Nothing touches us that God does not see. He already knows what will happen to us in life. No darkness is too dark for Him. He sees as clearly in the dark times as He does in the not-so-dark times. He is never surprised. Hebrews 4:13 tells us He knows about everyone everywhere. Everything about us is open to His all-seeing eyes. We can tell Him our pain, and we can ask for His help because He and He alone is the only one who can heal our deepest hurts.

When life takes a part of us, He is there! When the nights are lonely, and it seems like day will never come, He is there. When we have questions, and wonder why, He is there. There is never a moment in our life that He is not there. Just think, whether we are aware of His presence or not, He is there bringing us through. Psalm 34:18 says, "The Lord is nigh unto them that are of a broken heart; and saveth such as be of a contrite spirit."

22

Learning from Our Pain

Pain can leave us bitter or better. I am determined by God's grace to use my pain to be a better servant of God, a better me, a better friend, and a better parent. Realizing how quickly our lives can change, I am living each day with new goals in my life. I hope that by sharing them with you, it will help you as you begin to rebuild your life and to perhaps honor the one who is no longer with you or whatever has caused your pain.

We all have past sins and regrets. As long as we live in these earthly bodies, we will fail. I have many times over. If I had known my husband was going to die that day, I would have said no to his exercise that morning; I would have taken him to the hospital and spent all night at the hospital with him, but I did not have that; he left so quickly. He was ready to go even if I was not ready for him to leave. Perhaps God lets us remember these times so that the memory of past failures will cause us to turn the future into a life more fruitful and dedicated to Him and to others who are still with us.

God is a loving and forgiving God, and even though there may be things we wish we could do over, we need to leave with God our past and trust Him for our future. Do not let the "if onlys" destroy the wonderful memories you have and the goals you now have. The evil one is always trying to take from us the peace in our hearts that Jesus offers. Do not let these thoughts destroy that within you. Our life now may not be the life we dreamed of having, but it is the only life we will have on this earth, and we need to make the best of it until that day God calls us home to that new life with Him.

Because of My Pain

1. I am determined to be thankful for what I have and not be so concerned about what I do not have.
2. I have determined to cherish each moment God gives me. I want to invest my life in living and cherishing people. I want to tell everyone I am with how much God loves them and that He is with us in any pain we may go through in life.
3. I want my family, friends, and loved ones to remember me as someone who loved God, who was fun to be with, and who cared deeply for them.
4. I understand that life is so short. I do not want to look back at whatever life I have left and feel I wasted my time here on earth.
5. I want to do all I can, when I can, with all I can for my family and others.
6. I want to spend more time enjoying life, laughing much. I know there is pain, physical and emotional, but there is also much to be happy about.
7. I want to take more time just thanking God for my blessings and for His love for me.
8. I realize how unimportant "things" are. When we are coming to the end of life, we realize just how good God has been to us.
9. I understand that there is nothing here on earth I can take with me when I die. I want to do all I can to tell others how to go to heaven and live forever. Things fade away; love does not. Love is eternal.
10. I want to spend more time looking for those who are hurting and to be an encouragement to others. People are hurting, and I want to help them.

11. I determine to be more thankful for each breath God allows me to take and for my health; it can change in a second.

12. I will be more patient with others and less critical and be quick to forget and forgive those who are unkind to me.

13. I choose to move forward in my life. Often we find ourselves in places we do not want to be in. Instead of wondering why, I want to press on and go on from where I am now.

14. I want to cherish and believe what Jesus says in His word about faith, love, and His willingness to take care of all my needs. I want to understand His comfort in times of sickness and trouble and to trust His promises to be there with me, never to leave or forsake me, no matter what or where I am in life.

15. I want to pray for those God puts on my heart and love Jesus more every day.

23

Joy Is on the Way

The heartaches and pain we have in this world are just for a time. Christ's resurrection gives us hope and assurance of heaven, where we will live in the presence of God and with those who have gone on ahead. Knowing our loved one is absent here but is with the Lord comforts those of us who remain until that time comes for us to leave. Revelation 21:1–4 says,

> And I saw a new heaven and a new earth: for the first heaven and the first earth were passed away; and there was no more sea. And I John saw the holy city, new Jerusalem, coming down from God out of heaven, prepared as a bride adorned for her husband. And I heard a great voice out of heaven saying, Behold, the tabernacle of God is with men, and He will dwell with them, and they shall be his people, and God himself shall be with them, and be their God. And God shall wipe away all tears from their eyes; and there shall be no more pain: for the former things are passed away.

Knowing that Paul has found the fullness of life he preached about and longed for gives me strength to go on. Our home will never be the same without him, but we know we will be with him again. Our comfort comes from the one who gave His Son for our sins. He knows and understands what we are going through. As our spiritual growth does not just happen overnight, and neither does the process of our grief, but there is help for the Christian who is suffering. Hebrews 4:14–16 declares,

> Seeing then that we have a great high priest, that is passed into the heavens, Jesus the Son of God, let us hold fast our profession. For we have not an high priest which cannot be touched with the feeling of our infirmities; but was in all points tempted like as we are, yet without sin. Let us therefore come boldly unto the throne of grace, that we may obtain mercy, and find grace to help in time of need.

We never know how our pain may someday be used for others. What many may not know is that Handel's *Messiah* and the "Hallelujah Chorus" came at a time in Handel's life when he thought all was lost because of a stroke that left him in poor health, depressed, and all alone. He had once been a great musician, but now he felt that was all over and he had nothing to give. One day a friend sent him some mail that included some scriptures he thought Handel might put to music. Handel began to read: "And God shall wipe away all tears," and "The kingdoms of this world shall be for ever and ever," and other scriptures from the Old and New Testaments. Music and words began to come to his mind, and he begin to write *The Messiah*. Out of his loneliness and pain came the great "Hallelujah Chorus." When this was first performed, the king of England was so moved that he stood to his feet. Today when it is performed, you will see crowds of people standing to their feet out of respect for God, crying, and raising their hands in praise. All of this came out of the pain of one man who thought all was lost. I wonder what God can do in my and your life if we allow Him to use our pain to help others.

Most of us can quote the twenty-third Psalm about the Lord being our Shepherd, but the fourth verse has brought a new meaning to me. "Yea, though I walk *through* the valley of the shadow of death, I will fear no evil: for thou art with me; thy rod and thy staff, they comfort me." I begin to see the words like *walk through*; when we are walking, we are still going on, even though the steps may be hard and slow. Then there is the statement, "I will fear no evil: for thou art with me." I may not understand all that is going on, but God is with me in my pain and because of that, I can go on. When we think the tears will never stop, He gives us strength to keep walking on. And then, one day you wake up and you have a joy in your heart, the sun is shining through your window, and you begin to make plans for what you will do that day. You are thankful to God that He comforted you and kept you "walking through" the hardest time of life, step by step, however long it took. No matter how hard your pain is, do not give up; keep walking on. Someday you will look back and realize that in the hardest of times there was someone walking with you and helping you go on. You thought you could not take another step, but you did. There was someone helping you in your deepest pain, and that someone was Jesus.

Because of what you have been through, you now have more faith, and the words, "I will fear no evil: for Thou art with me" have new meaning. You saw that you did make it through the roughest time of your life. Strength you did not know you had was there, and you can help others by telling them when you thought you could not go another step, you found strength to go on. It was hard and the pain was real, but you got through it.

I am learning through my pain, even more now, that I can trust God to see me through whatever is going on in my life because He was there at a time when my heart was broken. No one gets through life without pain, but when we allow God to walk with us, we can and will come through. God is the only one who can see our fears, our pain, our doubts, and He is the only one that can provide the cure. We do not have all the answers, and we cannot see the end of our pain like God can, but listen to what Jeremiah 29:11 says: "For I know the thoughts that I think toward you saith the LORD. thoughts of peace, and not of evil, to give you an expected end." We have a new world awaiting us, and the problems and pain of this life will someday be gone forever. Isaiah

26:4 says, "Trust ye in the Lord for ever: for in the Lord JEHOVAH is everlasting strength." Our strength comes from the Lord.

In the meanwhile, God wants us to trust Him and know that as long as we are here on this earth, He is with us and will give us His strength as we face the hurts of life. We are not promised a life free of pain and suffering, but we are promised that God will be with us in whatever pain we have to go through in life. He knows it is painful, but He also knows His grace is sufficient.

24

Scriptures—and My Response

Joshua 1:9: Have I not commanded thee? Be strong and of good courage; be not afraid, neither be thou dismayed; for the LORD thy God is with thee whithersoever thou goeth.

My Response: Lord, I want to be strong in my loneliness and pain. I know You are with me, but I am missing my husband, and the pain is so deep.

Jeremiah 33:3: Call unto me, and I will answer thee, and shew thee great and mighty things which thou knoweth not.

My Response: Lord, You are the only one that I can call on for the strength I so need; please show me what to do.

Psalm 143:8: Cause me to hear thy loving kindness in the morning; for in thee do I trust; cause me to know the way wherein I should walk; for I lift up my soul unto thee.

My Response: Dear Lord Jesus, I need to hear Your voice and to know where I am to go and what I am to do now that Paul has gone to be with You.

> Deuteronomy 31:6: Be strong and of a good courage, fear not, nor be afraid of them: for the LORD thy God, he it is that doth go with thee; he will not fail thee, nor forsake thee.

My Response: God, thank You that when You came for Paul, he did not struggle and showed no fear but went right with You. I will never forget the look of peace on his face when he left me. I know You are with me now in my grief.

> Isaiah 25:8: He will swallow up death in victory; and the Lord GOD will wipe away tears from off all faces, and the rebuke of his people shall He take away from off all the earth: for the LORD hath spoken it.

My Response: Paul will never have to face death again. Thank You, God.

> John 14:1–3: Let not your heart be troubled, ye believe in God, believe also in Me. In My Father's house are many mansions; if it were not so I would have told you. I go to prepare a place for you and if I go to prepare a place for you, I will come again and receive you unto myself; that were I am there ye may be also.

My Response: Thank You, Lord, for this promise; I have such peace in knowing Paul is where You are and that someday I too will be with You and him forever.

> Psalm 55:22: Cast thy burden upon the LORD, and He shall sustain; he shall never suffer the righteous to be moved.

My Response: Lord, I cast all my burdens for my family, my life, everything on the one and only one who can bear all my burdens now and forever.

> Isaiah 41:10: Fear thou not; for I am with thee: be not dismayed for I am thy God: I will strengthen thee, yea, I will help thee, yea, I will uphold thee with the right hand of righteousness.

My Response: Thank You, God, for all these promises to care for me and so many more promises in Your word. I am secure in Your care. I trust You completely.

> 1 Thessalonians 4:13: But I would not have you to be ignorant, brethren, concerning them which are asleep, that ye sorrow not, even as others which have no hope.

My Response: Thank You, Lord, that I have the blessed hope of seeing my husband again. My grief is not without hope.

There are so many more scriptures I could quote that have helped me. I have almost filled a little notebook with the promises and my responses. You may want to do something like this or have your own way of responding to the many promises of God. Some may feel this is all foolishness and that God is not real. All I can say is that someday they will believe it. The Bible tells us that there will come a time when every knee will bow before Him and worship Him. I cannot imagine what that will be like, but I believe it!

Do not give up. God still has a work for us to do for Him. Draw close to God; He is there. He is going through this with you, but the difference is He knows what is ahead of our grief and suffering; we do not.

When Jesus was on the cross and cried out, "My God, My God why hast thou forsaken Me?" He felt the separation from His Father. This tells me He knows our pain and grief in being separated from the one we love, whether it be by death, Alzheimer's, divorce, or any separation. But we have the grave and the resurrection of Jesus to comfort our heart and soul. We have a life ahead of us forever.

Psalm 145:18 tells us God is near to all them that call upon Him. Keep praying, keep trusting, and keep asking. He hears, and He is there. Psalm 23 tells us that no matter where we have to walk in life, God is there, especially in the hardest and most severe times.

Yes, we will get through this and joy will come because we have a God who loves us and is with us.

25

Will I Ever Be Me Again?

Your pain may be so great right now that you wonder if you will ever be the same again; you probably will not. No matter what has caused your pain, you are a different person. Oh, the pain will get better, especially when you allow God to enter into your pain, but as far as being who you were before, I do not think so. There will always be that "missing" person in your heart whether it be because of death or some other loss. Love never leaves our heart. We will go on and continue to live, but what their leaving has taught us will make us better than ever before because of having them in our life.

It takes time to heal, but if you believe and trust in God, you will awaken one day and realize you have come through this pain and you have learned lessons you never learned before. There was someone all along with you, guiding you and helping you. Those times when we thought our hearts would break, He was there; when we thought we would never laugh again, He was there. When the memories were all we had left, He was there all along, giving us the strength to go on.

Through our hurt, God shows us how we can give help to others who are hurting and facing a pain that may be different from ours, but we can share with them that joy does come. The sun will shine again for you. My prayer through my pain is that my girls and I will come to know God in a greater way and be used of Him to help others, to glorify God, and to honor the memory of my husband and their dad.

Although most of my time has been spent on getting through the death of a loved one, I realize there are many different pains others are going through: losing the home one has worked for many years to build, loss of a job, the heartbreak of divorce, or any other pain. Life here on earth brings heartache to all of us. No matter who we are, known or unknown, rich or poor, sooner or later heartache comes to everyone. But God is still the same, no matter what we are going through. Through our pain, we feel the pain and hurt of others. If we as humans can feel like that, how much more the Father feels for us in our pain.

How do we go about putting our life back together again after it has been torn apart? Some may feel they are strong and grit their teeth and go on, but sooner or later that strong person will be left with an empty space in his or her heart that only God can fill. God is not caught off guard by what is happening in our lives, and He knows how to help us most. He is all-knowing and all-powerful. He is really the only one who knows what we are going through; no one else truly does. Just think of John 3:16: "For God so loved the world, that he gave his only begotten Son, that whosoever believeth in Him should not perish, but have everlasting life." God gave His only begotten Son for me and for you. Truly He is a God of love, love like we have never known. Only God can see the inside of us and where we need help most.

I do not know what your pain is, but I know this: we are not alone in our pain. I have learned that there is someone who is walking alongside of me and within me, no matter what. Do not give up. Anyone can give up; going on is what is hard. And as far as our grieving, to me it is a sign of our love for the one we have had to say good-bye to for the time being. That too has helped me, knowing my grieving is a sign of the love I have for my husband.

Even though our loved ones who have died are no longer here with us, the memory and the influence they had on our life and heart will never leave us. Because of that memory, I still feel my husband's presence in my life, and until the day I die, I hope to have the mind and heart to pass on to his children and grandchildren the kind of man he was and the legacy he has left behind for them to follow.

The pain of loss may be with us for a long time, but when we truly believe and put our trust in the one and only true God, we can count on it; we will smile again, and the sun will shine again for us. Joy will come again. God can do this! Just think of what Jesus did while He was on earth: He healed the sick, walked on water, made the wind and waves to cease, and died so that we could have life everlasting; then He rose again from the grave and is alive forevermore. If He can do this and so much more, He can take care of me and what I am going through. I had to ask myself this question: "Am I going to look to God for all that lies ahead for me, or am I going to fold up and quit?"

When I stood at my husband's casket, I knew it was the last time I would see his face here on earth. I did not want to leave, but I knew when I walked away it was just a matter of time and I would see him again like never before. I placed my hand on his heart and said, "Thank you, honey, for taking care of me," and I walked away. There was such a peace in my heart for the one who had cared for me and loved me for almost forty-nine years. I was not worthy of that love and failed many times, but he still loved me. Today, there is one who has loved and cared for me for seventy-five years, and I know with all my heart He is not going to fail me. I thank God for taking care of me. I walked away from my husband's body but not from the care of God.

What will I do now? How will I go on? Where will I look for comfort, security, love, and companionship? Where will I go for all that I found in my husband? Early in our ministry, it seemed like he was always putting the work of God first with the church and missions. Many times when funds were low in the church, he would not take a paycheck or take money we had set aside and give it to support the Bible ministry. One time, in my human flesh I said, "What will happen to me if something happens to you? Who will take care of me and the girls?" His reply was one that has carried me through our many years together. He calmly said, "You will be okay the day I die if God doesn't die also!" He knew I would be cared for in the best way. Today, the one I looked to as my earthly leader may have died, but the God he loved and served is still alive, and our family will look to Him for all we need. I know the God my husband trusted in all our years together will never leave or forsake me. What will I do? I will continue and look to God until that day when once again our family will be reunited forever with the Lord we all love and serve.

26

Notes to Joan

Through our suffering, we learn to place a greater value on love for family and people. We will never be the same again. We are awakened to how quickly life can change and what truly matters most to us. The life we had before is being replaced with the life we have now, and perhaps through this we learn and see that all we have is right now. The past is just that—the past. It will never come again. But we have today to make a difference in our own life and the lives of those around us. We are more sensitive to the pain of others because of the pain we have gone through.

My life has taken a different turn from the one I thought would be with Paul. I did not plan for it to change, but God knew what was ahead for me. Each day the pain of his not being here with us becomes a little less, and I can look back now and say you can trust God because I have felt and known His help when I needed it most. I had a thought the other day: Perhaps this is the weakest and strongest time of my life. I may not always know what to do about certain things now without Paul, but this I do know, there is One who knows, and in my weakness, I can put my trust in Jesus to meet my every need. I do not know what the next day may bring to my heart and life, but God does.

Tears can wash away a lot of who we were, where we failed, and open our eyes to the present and those around us. Life brings good and bad into our lives, but God can use us in both. Through our pain, we feel the pain and hurt others are feeling. God is the only one who can comfort best in our time of need; whether we believe it, or feel it, He is with us in every heartache. He can restore that aching and hurting heart.

The night Paul passed away, I said to my daughter Renee', "What will I do? He took care of so many things for me that I know nothing about." She was gone for a short time and came back and said, "Mom, you have nothing to worry about." She had looked in his computer and found a document titled "Notes to Joan" instructing me on what to do in case he went to heaven before me. He had written these down for me to find after he was gone. I have followed these notes and have been able to do things I never thought I could do.

God has written "notes to you and me" in His word, and we have nothing to worry about when we follow them. He also left His Holy Spirit within us when He left to be with His Father until He will once again return in clouds of glory to bring us to live with Him forever. He will guide us step by step in how we are to live and handle the pains of life. He is with us and will take care of us. We just need to believe the truth of God's word and not our feelings. Have faith! Psalm 46:10 tells us to "Be still and know that I am God." When the pain seems more than you can bear, just be still and know that God is with you and everything is all right when He is there. He has not failed us yet, and He never will. Your pain will get better. Psalm 30:5 tells us that "weeping may endure for a night but joy cometh in the morning." We can count on that. Each day is brighter, and joy does come.

It is my hope that because of our pain, we will look at life and those around us differently and cherish the moment we have and be grateful to God for His mercy and grace. We can trust God. I hope everyone reading this knows how much God loves you and has received Him as their Lord and Savior. If not, I pray you will ask the Lord Jesus to come into your heart and life right now. First John 1:9 says, "If we confess our sins He is faithful and just to forgive us our sins and to cleanse us from all unrighteousness."

There is no sin too great that God cannot and will not forgive.

Whenever I would ask his forgiveness for something I may have said or done, Paul would always say, "Of course I will forgive you." If a human can do that, how much more will God forgive us? This is something I can share with everyone. When we sincerely look to God and ask for His forgiveness, we too can know that all is forgiven. When God forgives us of our sins, no matter how bad we think they are or we have been, they are forgiven to be remembered no more and are removed as far as the east is from the west, never to be brought up again.

We will have other pains to go through in life. Even though the pain will hurt, and it may even be a greater pain, we know we can trust God to see us through.

27

Looking to What You Can't See

In Second Corinthians 4:18 we read, "While we look not at the things which are seen, but at the things which are not seen: for the things which are seen are temporal; but the things which are not seen are eternal."

Oh, dear one, read the above verse over and over. We look at what is going on now in our life and we may wonder if we will ever get through it, or if the pain will ever go away. The pain is real. I know that for sure. But I also know that God knows, and He is with us right now and in any pain that lies ahead. Our strength comes from Him. Second Corinthians 4:16 says: "For which cause we faint not; but though our outward man perish, yet the inward man is renewed day by day." It may seem like the pain will never go away, but do not give up; our strength is being renewed day by day. What may seem like a trial that will never end will someday be over, and it will seem as if it was a light affliction compared to what awaits us. We can only see the now; God sees the end of our life. Second Corinthians 4:17 says: "For our light affliction, which is but for a moment, worketh for us a far more exceeding and eternal weight of glory."

Satan gets in our minds and does not want us to believe in a God that is with us right now in our pain and will be with us forever. Second Corinthians 4:4 says, "In whom the gods of this world hath blinded the minds of them which believe not, lest the light of the glorious gospel of Christ who is the image of God, should shine in them." We must not allow the evil one to get into our minds and make us doubt all the promises we have that are ours now and forever. Second Corinthians 5:7 says, "For we walk by faith, not by sight." By faith, we trust in what we cannot see now but what is ours to come.

When I look back to the day my husband went to be with the Lord, and then look now at all God has brought me through, I cannot praise Him enough. Some people are going through persecutions and pains that most of us will never know or could never even imagine. Because of my pain, I have a greater desire to pray more fervently for those who are suffering, even those I may never meet this side of heaven.

We never lose our loved ones. Daily as I see my husband's face in pictures I have displayed in our home and in the eyes of our children and grandchildren, I see some of who he was. But I know that someday I will see him again like never before. He is away from us for now, but because I believe God and what His word tells me, I will be with him again someday. His leaving us is not the end of our life together. He has just gone on to that everlasting life that someday will be mine also. The picture of Paul on the next page says to me, "Good-bye for now. I'll see you again"

The best is yet to be! Our pain will not last forever. If I believed that death was the end of my life and the life of those I love, that would be the worst pain in all the world. But because I know it is just the beginning of a new life forever with my resurrected Lord and those who have gone on before, it makes the burdens of this life easier to bear. How thankful I am for God's word telling me over and over of His love for me, His death for me, and His paying the price for my sins so that I might live forever. What a price He paid for a sinner like me—His life for mine! Psalm 116:15 states, "Precious in the sight of the LORD is the death of his saints."

During revival services one year a church member asked, "Pastor, what should be the result in my life from these services?" His reply was, "We should come to know Christ better!" As he thought upon his answer, God gave him the words and music to "Just to Know Him."

Just to Know Him

In this life so filled with misery and woe,
There is someone who you really need to know

How He died on Calvary to set you free
And to save your soul for all eternity.

Our life is filled with many goals and aims
And so many seeking vain and fleeting fame.
Now for us there is a goal that tops them all,
Just to know the Christ who keeps us from the fall.

In this world so filled with misery and woe,
There is one who surely can defeat our foe.
I will live to tell the story of His love,
How He came one day to save me for above.

We truly have a story now to tell,
How that souls can go to heaven and not to hell,
For His wondrous grace is given to all men,
And for this the Father Christ to earth did send.

To know the one who really makes us whole,
For revival there is surely this one goal,
Just to know the Christ who promised to be near
And whose presence drives away our every fear.

Chorus

Just to know Him, just to know Him,
Just to know the one who die to set me free.
Just to know Him, just to know Him,
Just to know the One who lives eternally.

Words By: Pastor Paul R. Knierim
Music By: Mary Renee' (Gamble) Knierim

After seventy-five years of life, I am more convinced than ever that
the greatest need of every person alive is to really know Jesus—to know
God is truly the greatest thing that will ever happen to us. But how

do I get to know someone I cannot see physically? When we read the complete biblical history of how God created the heavens and the earth, how He sent Jesus to be born of a virgin, how He came and walked and lived as a person among people, and how He gave His life for sinners like me, we can then see and know God because of what we know about Jesus. Jesus said, "I and my Father are one" (John 10:30).

When you and I go through the trials of life, God gives us peace, a peace that passes all understanding. He can quiet our hearts and souls and help us as we begin to rebuild our lives from whatever has caused our pain.

Found in My Husband's Computer after He Was Gone

Thoughts on The Way to Heaven
by Pastor Paul R. Knierim, DD
(In his own words)

During the course of one's life, millions of thoughts are contemplated by the mind. I have undertaken to record some of mine that I consider to be of a more noteworthy nature than the rest. This compilation is in no particular order or systematic arrangement. I simply listed them as I thought of them. Some of them are borrowed from others, some are adaptations of ideas shared by others, and some are original with me. Perhaps one or more may be of interest or value to you the reader. I undertook to record them because I had a thought that they were of value.

As a born-again Christian, I am on my way to heaven. The journey has many blessings and trials, which can be said of all saints. My experiences are certainly not unique. Most of my thoughts aren't either. However, I may have had one or two original thoughts along the way that will help and inspire my fellow travelers. (At least it can be recorded that my brain did function on occasion.)

1. We minister to others best through our own wounds.
2. All that you do, do with eternity in mind.

3. Our prayer should be: "Lord, make me holy."

4. Everyone God saves, He changes.

5. Testing is designed by God for the strengthening of faith.

6. Give to others, and expect from God.

7. Entrust to God what you have; trust God for what you need.

8. The Bible is a record of God answering prayers.

9. The more you say, the more chance to say something wrong.

10. Satan seeks to rob us of our spiritual hungers.

11. If you live for God, you can't lose. If you live for self, you can't win.

12. Obey God and trust God for the results.

13. Disobedience is a harsher teacher than obedience.

14. Today is the future you worried about yesterday.

15. To share in His glory, I must first share in His sufferings.

16. God is *enough* (Phil. 4:19)!

17. Don't ask God for something you don't really want or believe He will do.

18. Continued need requires continued prayer.

19. Prayer: Man's ultimate contribution to the furtherance of God's work.

20. Be persistent in prayer to obtain faith that receives from God.

21. The happiest person is he or she who is content with the least.

22. Sinful behavior is living independently of God.

23. Faith in God is greater riches than gold (I Peter 1:7).

24. All we will not let go of returns to poison us.

25. Hope is sorrow's adorning.

26. God loves our children more than we do; trust Him!

27. The pastor's family is more intensely attacked by Satan.

28. Revival: God's ongoing desire for and work in believers.

29. We go to church to worship God.

30. Relationship is the key to discipleship.

31. I long for holiness!

32. To repent is to confess and forsake sin.

33. Memory is a God-given gift intended to be an aid to faith.

34. Music was given by God to man for the purpose of praising God.

35. Don't ask God to bless you; obey God and He *will* bless you.

36. If you are not praying, what are you doing?

37. Our biggest battles are not with the devil but with ourselves and God.

38. Meekness is submission.

39. Be right and you'll do right.

40. If God played favorites, I could be out of favor.

41. The essence of God's will is being what we should be more than doing what we should do.

42. Be glad to suffer for God and His church (Col. 1:24).

43. It costs to do right, but it costs more to do wrong.

44. The main thing is to keep the main thing the main thing.

45. Focus on problems—no peace. Focus on Christ—know peace.

46. God gives us needs to remind us of our need for Him (John 15:5).

47. God expects a holy life from those to whom He has given His Holy Spirit.

48. Live today!

49. I'm not lucky; I've been graced by God!

50. To live by faith, make sure your life is pleasing to God every day.

51. True preaching is the result of a living relationship between God and His servant.

52. Joy is Jesus, not new circumstances.

53. The secret of abiding is dying.

54. God leads us to pray for what is on His heart.

55. God loves our children more than we do.

56. Better to be silent and thought a fool than to speak and remove all doubt.

57. God saves us to serve, and our primary service is *prayer.*

58. Troubles are investments for eternal glory.

59. If we knew everything, we would lose the joy of learning.

60. Leave God out and we are left with nothing.

61. The willingness to be a nobody for God makes one a somebody. The desire to be somebody is to be on the road of becoming a nobody.

62. The pain of sin is always greater than the pleasure of sin.
63. They say seeing is believing, but many saw the miracles of Jesus and never believed.
64. God *alone* leads to faith that leads to *triumph*.
65. It has been said, "A person is only as good as his word." Well, God is good and so is His word. God is good because He keeps His word, and God keeps His word because He is good!

There were many more of his thoughts listed, which shows a man whose thoughts were on God and doing right.

In going through his files, I found where he had written his thoughts on many subjects.

I thought of the verse in Hebrews 11:4: "By faith, Abel offered unto God a more excellent sacrifice than Cain, by which he obtained witness that he was righteous, God testifying of his gifts: and by it *he being dead yet speaketh.*" My husband may no longer be here, but the life and the words he left behind speak for him.

Revelation 14:13 says, "And I heard a voice from heaven saying unto me, Write, Blessed are the dead which die in the Lord from henceforth: Yea, saith the Spirit, that they may rest from their labours; and their works do follow them."

28

A Life Changed

Change can bring heartache or joy, but it does mean leaving what was once the life we had and going on to what now is. Because of the changes we have gone through, life will never be the same again; however, how we allow these changes to affect our life is so important. As we begin to adjust to this new way of life (no matter what has caused our pain), we begin to get back to who we were and hopefully a better us. Be patient; change of any kind does not just happen overnight, and it may take longer than you want. Hopefully, because of what you have been through, you are not only a better person, but you appreciate life in a greater way than ever before.

After Paul went to be with the Lord, there was less for me to do. So much of our life was together, but now it was just me. After about a year I realized I had to find new ways to invest my time. I began to pray and ask God to show me how I could be a blessing and not a burden. Nothing can ever replace the one who is absent, and the memories they left behind will be ours forever, but I knew he would not want me to fold up and quit; I also knew this was not God's will for me. I asked God to show me how I could be used to honor Him and my husband. The ways have been numerous. As long as we are alive, there is something for all of us to do, and God will show us and put things and people in our life we would never have thought of on our own. This too is a great part in our healing.

As I have said, my husband's later years were spent in much prayer. To him it was a ministry. There is a price to pay, and I believe the hardest and greatest work of all is intercessory prayer, setting yourself apart from the world and others and spending hours alone with God. This is not neglecting those in your life. It never interfered with my husband doing the things he liked to do and spending time with our family. We all have special memories of the good times we had together, but we also have memories of Paul spending time in prayer when we were all off doing something else. We later would go looking for him and find him in his lounge chair with open Bible in hand. His trust was in the God he knew and who kept his heart and soul at rest no matter what was happening around him. The day he died, I pulled his head close to me, trying to help him breath, but he heard a voice I could not hear, and he left without any struggle whatsoever with what he was leaving behind.

Too often we may fail to see that right in the midst of us may be one who walks with God as much as the great saints of old. We need to learn from them how to live well and die well. My husband was one of them, and not until God took him home did I fully realize the impact his prayers had on so many.

I wonder if people who lived in the days of those who are considered great saints of the past recognized the way history records their presence here on earth. Did their friends and families see them as they are portrayed today or just as who they were to them? Even today it may be unknown to many who the great saints truly are. It may be a missionary who is on the mission field or some godly pastor of a small church in the back woods somewhere giving his all to God and others.

I have received letters from many saying, "I wish I had told your husband the impact he had on my life." With me was a man who gave himself to God as much as any man could. What is sad is that far too often we do not see what and who people were for God until they are gone. If someone is alive today and has made an impact on your life for good, tell him or her now. Do not wait until it is too late, and you wish you had.

One of the most widely read devotional books today is Oswald Chambers' *My Utmost for His Highest*. Millions of people all over the world read this classic devotional every day. What many do not know is that Oswald Chambers did not write it. At the end of the foreword of that devotional, one may see the letters B.C. Who was this? It was his wife. Oswald Chambers was with the Lord, and these devotionals were taken from the teachings he had given to the students at the Bible Training College. Because she did not give up after his death, this book is still one of the most sought-after devotionals. People who have never read it are still discovering it for the first time. Oswald Chambers went to be with the Lord over a hundred years ago, yet his work is still following after him because of a wife who would not give up.

29

Cherish the Moment

This moment is all that we have, and we need to cherish it now. We must tell those in our lives what they mean to us now, learn to forgive now, and turn loose of those things that are tearing us apart. Do not trust in and cherish "things," but rather trust in God and cherish our loved ones. The evil one wants to destroy us and all we hold dear because he knows who God is and the great love He has for us.

If I hear there is a storm coming and the electricity may be off, I prepare in advance for what may happen. I get out the flashlights and candles, make sure my cell phone is charged, make sure there is food and water in the house, and do any other necessary preparations to ensure that I am ready for the moment when the electricity goes off. We do not know what may happen tomorrow, and we need to prepare today to love and to enjoy the blessings God has given us. I have failed so many times in the past to heed this warning. I do not want to miss out on the joy that is mine today and fail to do what I can do now. None of us know how the next second, minute, or day may happen to change our life forever.

My husband used to say to me he wanted to do what he could for our girls while he was alive so he could see them enjoy the gift. Our daughters and grandkids have memories of a grandfather who was willing to do what he could for them while he was still here with them.

He left a legacy of a father who gave of himself here on earth to care and provide for his children, and he left them with a memory of a godly dad who taught them the value of service to God and others. If there is someone God places on your heart to do something for, do it; that way that person and you can receive the joy of the gift.

Maybe it is hard for you to say, "I love you," or tell others what they mean or have meant to you. Do not wait until it is too late; say today what you need to say. This can be the road to healing for you and for them. Life has to be lived in the *now*; that is where we are. God works with us in the *now* of our life to bring us to where He can use us to glorify Him, and yes, that can mean in the hard times as well as the good times.

It took the pain of my broken heart to understand more fully the pain of others in a way like I never have before. We never know how our pain will be used in our life and the life of another. I always had compassion and sympathy when someone was hurting or suffering, but I now look deeper into the face of a stranger I may meet, a friend or loved one, or someone who may be many countries away from me, and my heart is linked with that person's heart. Perhaps all along this is what God intended for our pain to do. We become more compassionate, more kind and loving, and more determined to not make the same mistakes we have made in the past and to reach out to others with a heart of love and understanding.

I have opened my heart and shared much about the man I was married to, my grieving, things that have helped me, how to help others, and how to begin rebuilding your life, but nothing I have said or can say will heal our pain like the help that comes from God. I wish I had words now to say how wonderful His grace is to us. If I wanted any one thing accomplished in sharing my heart, it would be to tell others *cherish the moment with God most especially and every moment you have now with your loved ones. The Bible is the greatest book we will ever hold in our hands, and it is the only book that can truly change our heart because it is God speaking to us.* Do not neglect it, for truly that is one of the first steps in finding peace in our pain.

People come and go in our lives, but family, good or bad, is forever.

The evil one will do all he can to get into our minds, and he will do all he can to destroy us. Do not allow him to fill your mind with thoughts of where you think you failed. Think of all the things you *did* do right. God wants to come into our hearts and minds and give us peace in our pain. The life we are now living is not the end. That is a promise from God to all who have accepted Him as their Lord and Savior. *Someday we may find out that in the midst of our deepest pain, the beauty of Christ was shown to us and to others in ways we never thought possible.*

My husband always brought me roses. He planted several rose bushes just for me, but in every rose he gave me, there were thorns. Sometimes one would prick me and I would bleed, but it never stopped me from enjoying the roses. In all my pain, I can say without any hesitation that God loves me, cares for me, hears my cries and prayers, knows my pain, gives me strength, protects me, helps me with my burdens and weakness, is all goodness and mercy, is my Shepherd, is my Savior and my Lord, knows the number of hairs on my head, promises never to leave or forsake me no matter what is going on in my life, gives me wisdom, is my Helper, never sleeps or slumbers, is always faithful, forgives my sins, gives me peace in the storms and trials of life, gives strength in my weakness, knows all about me and still loves and renews me inside and out, and can do what no other one can do, for with God nothing is impossible. I am promised life with Him forever when I die. *He gave His life for mine. What more do I need when I have Jesus?*

Yes, we will get through the pain we now have. But we will have other pains as long as we live in this life. I cannot paint a perfect picture of a life free of pain when we trust God. One day we will exchange our trials here for peace forevermore. Changes will come, but the One who never changes will be there, all along, waiting for us to call out to Him and trust Him for all the burdens of our life. That is why He came, so that you and I might have the abundant life. In the twenty-third Psalm David said, "The Lord *is* my Shepherd," not *was* my Shepherd at one time, nor did the Psalmist say the Lord is my Shepherd only *if* I am deserving—no! He is our Shepherd right now, this moment, when we need Him, day or night; He is right there watching over us.

This is a lesson I learned from my husband. Anywhere Paul was, he was with God. It was not as if he always had to be away and shut up by himself. If we were just having time together, were out to eat, or with family, he was at peace with his God. I could walk into a room and say, "Are you ready to go to dinner?" He would say, "I'm ready!" He was almost like a child; he was content wherever he was because of his faith. I want to be like that. He never worried if people thought him to be out of touch with modern-day teachings. His preaching was never prepared to please the listener, for he was more concerned about being faithful to God than being popular with man. I miss getting up in the mornings and walking into his corner of the house and seeing him in his chair already talking to God before the day had begun for the rest of us.

The day Paul died I thought, *I don't know how to live without him.* My life changed, and the silence reminded me that he was no longer here in the flesh, but I could almost hear him say, "God is still with you." Pain is real; it hurts and changes our lives, but it does not have to destroy us. We do not know what tomorrow holds. We cannot know our future or know what will happen to us. Even if we could know, it would not take the pain away.

Just because we believe in God does not mean we will not have pain and heartache in life, but when our faith is in God, we have a strength and power to help us through whatever we have to face. It is not just something we talk about but something we can experience and know.

Sometimes out of the darkest days of our life may come the greatest blessings and treasures. We must never lose faith. We cannot see the future; God does and already knows what is ahead for us.

After my husband was gone, I began to look in his old computer. I found much that told me he knew he was going to heaven soon, even if I did not. So much of who he was and how he lived and thought was left behind for me to see and know that all was well with him and God.

Poems by Pastor Knierim

At Last
At last it's time for me to die
And take my journey to the sky.
No more sorrow, no more pain;
For me to die will be such gain.

No more bills and no more pills,
For I have looked unto the hills.
Christ is coming to take me home.
From His love, I will never roam.

Forever in Heaven
Forever in heaven I'll sing.
Praises to Jesus I will bring.
Oh, t'will be a wonderful thing
To kneel as I sing to my King.

To Jesus my King I shall sing
As praises to Him I shall bring.
When I kneel down at His throne,
I'll praise the oOne who my sins did atone

Oh, t'will be a wonderful thing
When I can kneel before my King.
Forever His praises I will sing
And make the courts of heaven ring.

This poem says a lot about him. Because he could no longer get on his knees when he prayed, one can feel the faith he had in knowing that someday he would be free from all sickness and pain and that he would be able to once again get on his knees to worship and honor the Lord he loved.

And then the singing! When the girls would play the piano and organ at home, and we all would sing, we always teased him because he did not care if he had the right words or the right tune; he just enjoyed making a joyful noise to the Lord. Whether we thought it was joyful or not, he enjoyed singing. Now he can sing to his heart's content.

The following poem is one that Paul wrote after his father died. We never knew he had written it until we found it in his computer.

A Tribute to My Dad
Paul Krueger Knierim

The example he set shall ever endure.
He has a family that loves him for sure;
Kitty and Kathy, Paul, and the rest.
He is my dad, and he *is* the best.

Renee' and Lynn and Rachel all three,
His pride in them was easy to see.
Michael and Mitchell, then Bethany too,
His joy in them everyone knew.

Joan, Tom, and David—he took to his heart,
Charles (Lauren and Morgan) though miles apart;
His treasure in life—his family though small,
But to us he gave his best and his all.

How happy in heaven—life's troubles are o'er.
On June 12 he sailed to the heavenly shore;
Someday I'll join him, and forever we'll be
Father and son—when again him I see.

A tower of strength while molding a son,
Now finished his race that was surely well run.
Sad that he's gone, but for this I am glad.
I'll never forget that he *is* my dad.

Paul joined his dad in heaven on November 28, 2015.

As I said earlier in this book, Paul was a man of prayer, and not only did his life show it, but now we are finding thoughts, poems, and notes that he wrote and left behind. These memories tell us more of who he was and what was on his heart and mind—God, family, and others. Two of the many short choruses he composed are as follows:

More Time for Prayer

More time for prayer,
Yes, more time for prayer.
You can show that you care,
And give more time to prayer.

More time for prayer,
Yes, more time for prayer.
In God's work you can share,
And give more time for prayer.

So Many Souls

So many souls that need to be won.
We must tell them today, for our work is not done.
Tell them of Jesus, the one who can save,
And of His blood, which He freely gave.

The following article was found in his files after he was gone to heaven.

Words of Life
By Dr. Paul R. Knierim

Name a book that never needs revision, is always true, and has been that way for hundreds of years. In addition, this book is always relevant, up to date, and has the answer to our every question concerning happy and successful living. There is *only one* such book—*the Bible*.

The Bible is a record of God's will and His workings. It gives us eternal truth and tells us how to be truly happy. The Bible is authored by God alone (through human writers), and thus it is unique among all books. Only those who know its contents can truly be said to be educated.

The Bible is powerful in its ability to both comfort and convict. It can educate and edify. Its words can regenerate our life and rebuke our lifestyle. Those who would be wise spend their life studying its teachings, which are both life giving and life enhancing.

When we possess a copy of God's word, we have in our possession the greatest literary masterpiece of all time. In studying it, we have an inexhaustible supply of daily help and blessing. By obeying it, we receive an eternity of God's loving care.

The Bible is a treasure house of truth, a collection of wise counsel, a history of God's holy acts, and literature detailing God's love.

Truly it can be said that *happiness is knowing and doing God's will* as revealed in the Bible!

When the medical staff was working with Paul and trying to help him, our daughter Renee' came over to me and knelt down by my chair and stayed with me. She stayed right by my side, and even though the tears were rolling down her cheeks and her heart was breaking, she would not leave me for one second. I believe God does that in a far greater way for us. He stays right with us, feels our pain, cries with us, and never leaves our side while we are suffering. At the time, I never thought of her on her knees watching out for me, but later I remembered this so plainly. She never left my side.

God is there with us. We may not remember it or even think of it at the time, but later we remember. Yes, He was there all along helping us through what we could have never gone through without Him. He said He would never leave or forsake us, and He stays right with us until we are okay again.

My main reason for writing this book was to help those who are suffering. The reader's pain may be totally different from mine, but the cure and help are the same. Because of my pain, I can feel the pain of others in a deeper way, but more importantly, God cares and He can do what no one else can do. He can take that broken heart and turn it into something beautiful. A broken heart can heal, and we learn to love and cherish those in our life like never before. We can rest assured there has not been one moment that God has left our side when we are going through the worst pain of our lives. Whether we feel it or not, He is there. Cherish the moment. That's all we have—this moment!

30

Blessed Promises from God's Word

Whatever has caused our pain, we all long for healing. Some will seek help from medicine or a counselor. No matter how good a counsellor or doctor may be, a broken heart must heal from the inside, and only God can see what is going on within us and can heal our broken heart.

Promises God Makes to Those Who Trust Him

1 Peter 5:7: Casting all you care upon him; for he careth for you.

Psalm 43:5: Why art thou cast down, O my soul? And why art thou disquieted within me? hope thou in God; for I shall yet praise him, who is the health of my countenance, and my God.

Psalm 23:4: Yea, though I walk through the valley of the shadow of death, I will fear no evil: for thou art with me; thy rod and thy staff they comfort me.

Psalm 34:18: The Lord is nigh unto them that are of a broken heart; and saveth such as be of a contrite sprite.

Isaiah 41:10: Fear thou not; for I am with thee: be not dismayed for I am thy God: I will strengthen thee; yea, I will help thee; yea, I will uphold thee with the right hand of my righteousness.

For Direction in Life

Isaiah 42:16: And I will bring the blind by a way they knew not; I will lead them in paths that they have not known: I will make darkness light before them, and crooked things straight. These things will I do for them and not forsake them.

Luke 1:79: To give light to them that sit in darkness and in the shadow of death, to guide our feet unto the way of peace.

Psalm 48:14: For this God is our God for ever and ever: he will be our guide even unto death.

Psalm 139:9–10: If I take the wings of the morning, and dwell in the uttermost parts of the sea; Even there shall thy hand lead me, and thy right hand shall hold me.

Psalm 32:8: I will instruct thee and teach thee in the way which thou shalt go; I will guide thee with mine eye.

Proverbs 3:5–6: Trust in the Lord with all thine heart, and lean not unto thine own understanding. In all thy ways acknowledge him, and he shall direct thy path.

Isaiah 30:21: And thine ears shall hear a word behind thee, saying, This is the way, walk ye in it, when ye turn to the right hand, and when ye turn to the left.

Nahum 1:7: The Lord is good, a strong hold in the day of trouble, and he knoweth them that trust in him.

John 14:18: I will not leave you comfortless: I will come to you.

Psalm 147:3: He healeth the broken in heart, and bindeth up their wounds.

Psalm 31:24: Be of good courage, and he shall strengthen your heart, all ye that hope in the Lord.

His Promise in the Loss of a Loved One

1 Thessalonians 4:13: But I would not have you to be ignorant, brethren, concerning them which are asleep, that ye sorrow not, even as others which have no hope.

Psalm 55:22: Cast thy burden upon on the Lord, and he shall sustain thee: he shall never suffer the righteous to be moved.

Isaiah 60:20: Thy sun shall no more go down; neither shall thy moon withdraw itself: for the Lord shall be thine everlasting light, and the days of thy mourning shall be ended.

Luke 6:21: Blessed are ye that hunger now, for ye shall be filled. Blessed are ye that weep now; for ye shall laugh.

Isaiah 25:8: He will swallow up death in victory: and the Lord God will wipe away tears from off all faces; and the rebuke of his people shall he take away from off all the earth: for the Lord hath spoken it.

First Corinthians 15:55, 57: O death, where is thy sting? O grave, where is thy victory? But thanks be to God, which giveth us the victory through our Lord Jesus Christ.

John 14:1–3: Let not your heart be troubled; ye believe in God, believe also in me. In my Father's house are many mansions: if it were not so, I would have told you. I go to prepare a place for you. And if I go and prepare a place for you, I will come again, and receive you unto myself, that where I am, there ye may be also.

John 14:18: I will not leave you comfortless: I will come to you.

John 14:27: Peace I leave with you, my peace I give unto you: not as the world giveth, give unto you. Let not your heart be troubled, neither let it be afraid.

These pages are to record your notes on how you were helped and your thoughts, memories, and pictures of your loved ones. This is your book to share your words and stories for those who follow after you. It is your book of healing.

What I Am Most Thankful For

1.

2.

3.

4.

5.

6.

7.

8.

9.

10.

11.

12.

13.

14.

15.

Your Thoughts and Memories

1.

2.

3.

4.

5.

6.

7.

8.

9.

10.

11.

12.

13.

14.

15.

Remembering the Good Times

When sad memories come to mind, recall some happy memories and write them down. Think on these things.

1.

2.

3.

4.

5.

6.

7.

8.

9.

10.

11.

12.

13.

14.

15.

My Favorite Snapshots

Things That Made Them Who They Were

Write Down Special Things They Said and Did

1.

2.

3.

4.

5.

6.

7.

8.

9.

10.

11.

12.

13.

14.

15.

Things You Never Want to Forget

1.

2.

3.

4.

5.

6.

7.

8.

9.

10.

11.

12.

13.

14.

15.

Things That Helped You Most

1.

2.

3.

4.

5.

6.

7.

8.

9.

10.

11.

12.

13.

14.

15.

What I've Learned through My Pain

1.

2.

3.

4.

5.

6.

7.

8.

9.

10.

11.

12.

13.

14.

15.

Extra Blank Pages

For Your Personal Thoughts

Extra Blank Pages

For Your Personal Thoughts

Bible Scriptures I Want to Remember

1.

2.

3.

4.

5.

6.

7.

8.

9.

10.

11.

12.

13.

14.

15.

16.

17.

18.

19.

20.

Thank You To

My daughter Lynn Kemp, who would not give up or give in until I put my thoughts to words about how others can be helped when they are going through the worst pain of their life and to know *"there was a man who lived on this earth and walked with God."* Also to my daughter Renee' Gamble for her expert proofreading and corrections and for always being there for me, and to my daughter Rachel Knierim for her encouragement always and for making me laugh when I needed it most.

To Jonathan and Kimberly Hedden for giving so much of their time in teaching me the computer techniques and to WestBow Press staff.

Most especially to those who will read this book. My desire is that you, whoever you are, will find the peace of God for this life and that the God of all comfort will bless you in whatever your pain may be. I may not know you now, but I will know you throughout all of eternity.

All scripture taken from the King James Version of the Bible.

EPILOGUE

Separation of any kind can be hard, but the separation of death is perhaps the hardest of all, especially when it is the death of one we loved and cherished here on earth. But even though that pain has left an empty spot in our hearts, we do learn to move on to the life that is ahead. We learn to cherish more deeply what we had and what we still have here in their memory and the life they left behind.

My main reason for writing this book was for others to know they are never alone in their pain. When our hearts are broken, we grieve. We are sad and we wonder if the pain will ever end. But it does, and when we look to God, we can come through a stronger person than ever before.

I have found help in my pain, and I want this for everyone who is hurting. I want this book to be something that will help them find the peace I have found, and this only takes time. God is with us every moment, and when we look to Him, He comforts us.

My life has changed from what I thought it would be. I must now look to the life that is ahead and allow God to use my pain to help others. I must not be sad. I have much to be happy about. Someday I will understand how the pain, as well as the happy times, was all woven together to make me who I am and who God intended me to be. I may not understand everything now, but I will someday. When we come to the times in our life where we need more strength, God is there. Often we worry about tomorrow and how we will get through it, when *God promises us His grace as we need it.* Words at the end of 1 Samuel 7:12, "Hitherto hath the Lord helped us," have encouraged me in getting through each day, each week, and each month. God is already in all my tomorrows, and as He helped me through the hard days before, He will be there for all the hard days ahead.

Life has its heartaches and fears, but we can face those fears and know God is stronger than anything we might have to go through. I am now travelling the road to who I am becoming for the remainder of my life. I want to make the journey, don't you? It's not what you and I can do, but what God can do.

Printed in the United States
By Bookmasters